£3

TALES
FROM AROUND THE WICKET

TALES
FROM AROUND THE
WICKET

told by
The Lord's Taverners

A Graham Tarrant Book
David & Charles
Newton Abbot   London

Picture acknowledgements
The Lord's Taverners and the Publishers gratefully acknowledge permission
to reproduce the following pictures:
Picture page 1 (*bottom*) The Kent Messenger; p2 (*bottom*)/p3 (*top*) Sport
& General; p3 (*bottom*)/p4 (*bottom*) The Photo Source. And to Roger Kemp
for all the photographs in the second picture section. Other pictures by
courtesy of the contributors.

'Test Debut' by Keith Andrew first appeared in *Wisden Cricket Monthly.*

British Library Cataloguing in Publication Data

Tales from around the wicket. – (A Graham
    Tarrant book]
    1. Cricket – Stones, anecdotes
    I. Lord's Taverners
    796.35'8

ISBN 0-7153-9190-9

Printed in Great Britain
by Billings & Sons Ltd Worcester
for David & Charles Publishers plc
Brunel House   Newton Abbot   Devon

CONTENTS

FOREWORD

In offering you *Tales from Around the Wicket*, I should like to say that this is the eleventh book we have published since the Charity began in 1950.

You will see from the list of contributors what a fabulous membership The Lord's Taverners enjoys. All these famous and successful cricketers have given their services absolutely free - Keith Miller and Greg Chappell even rang from Australia about their contributions! I should like to thank them all for their ready response to my appeal.

The idea of forming The Lord's Taverners was conceived outside the old Tavern at Lord's in 1950. Famous personalities decided to raise money for youth cricket for all the fun they had had in watching the game at Lord's. Today, our money for youth cricket is channelled through the National Cricket Association (the governing body of cricket outside the first-class game) and also the English Schools' Cricket Association. We provide artificial pitches, cricket equipment and coaching, and finance the largest cricket competition in the world, involving 1,500 schools (The Lord's Taverners Cricketer Colts Competition). Our objective in this competition is to encourage comprehensive schools to play cricket.

To publish a cricket book is a most natural thing for The Lord's Taverners to do. *Tales from Around the Wicket* is to be enjoyed story by story. All the royalties will be ploughed back into the coaching and development of young cricketers.

Anthony Swainson OBE
Director

A MAN TRUE TO HIS WORD
Tony Lewis

It was my first county match in Yorkshire. In the bus on the way up north there had been a lot of talk about J.C. Clay and how he used to say that he would never retire until Glamorgan had beaten Yorkshire in Yorkshire.

Alas! He had to. He played from 1921, when Glamorgan became first class, to 1949, when he retired, the year after our first County Championship title; but there was no joy for us in Yorkshire.

So Bradford Park Avenue was forbidding; a football stand on one side, concrete terracing around, a Wuthering Heights of a pavilion with dark dressing-rooms up on the first floor.

We arrived on the ground early to find lots of spectators already in their seats, or at least, if not sitting, having already staked out the vantage points with sandwich box, tea flask and the mackintosh. Veteran commissionaires in black uniforms, white peaked caps and shining brasses, barred entrances to almost everywhere until proper credentials were presented.

In the dressing-room I changed next to Alan Jones, Billy Davies and David Evans. You might describe Alan and me as novices and Billy and David as inexperienced. It was sprog corner.

Wilfred Wooller was not playing and so Gilbert Parkhouse was captain. As Gilbert went through the door to toss, in came Fred Trueman. Allan Watkins had warned us that he would be in.

'Spends more time in the opposing dressing-room than his own, but he's great fun as long as you don't let him frighten you. It's a bit green out there but he can only bowl at one end.'

Fred Trueman sat on a table rattling off hilarious jokes and sharp comments about players around the counties. Then he turned his stubbly Desperate Dan chin in our direction. When he saw such a cluster of beginners, his thick eyebrows shot up and stayed like a black lintel above two wide eyes; the voice was loud and nasal. It was as if the bull had spotted four schoolkids in the corner of a field and was pawing the ground and snorting at them.

Bernard Hedges introduced us. We shook the great fast bowler's hand.

He was now talking to nobody but us.

'I 'it Peter May on 'is 'ead last week, tha knows.'

Our mouths dropped open.

'Ay! An' that Colin Cowdrey ... ah'll tell thee: wun in t' block 'ole and wun in t'Adam's apple and it were a good day, sunshine.'

Mouths fell wider.

'Graveney! Thomas Graveney. E's a front foot player but 'ee never get's on front foot t'me, tha knows. Ee knows ah'd pin 'im like a moth t' bluddy sightscreen.'

We were instantly on the back foot, and still were minutes later when Gilbert Parkhouse returned.

'Sorry, chaps. We've lost it. Vic's put us in. It's a bit green but ... oh! Hello, Frederick.'

'Good day, Gilbert. Put you in 'as 'ee. Just like a bluddy batter. Na it's me who 'as t'bowl y'art, in't it?' He got up and pigeon-toed it towards the door and as we watched the large swaggering backside go, he was still regaling us. 'An' that Dexter, Lord Edward. 'Is bat's got more cracked edges than a broken piss-pot.'

He stopped and turned to us. 'Well, it's reet nice to welcome you young lads to cricket in Yorkshire. They call it the bull ring art there, don't they, Gilbert? Because I come down the 'ill from that 'igh red wall a bit sharpish.'

He went halfway through the door and turned yet again. 'Well good luck t'y'four. Ah'll see you all in t'middle, wun by bluddy wun.'

BEEN THERE DONE THAT
Ian Chappell

John 'Cho' Gleeson came to Test cricket via the country, where he spent most of his playing days as a wicket-keeper/batsman. Late in his cricket life (it could have been later than we knew because he never showed us his passport), he entered the Test arena as a folded-finger mystery spinner.

Even when he entered the hurly-burly of the Test arena John still retained his relaxed, country-boy attitude and this came in handy in moments of crisis . . .

Australia had come to Lord's one down in 1972, but was clawing it's way back into the series by putting up a good show in the second Test. We had bowled England out for 272 and in reply were 190 for four, with Greg Chappell and Ross Edwards having added 106 and looking in control. I hadn't thought about a night-watchman until a few minutes before stumps. Then, realising Rod Marsh had been our top scorer in the first Test, I figured he should be protected from the new ball that was due. Question was, who should protect him?

On gazing around the room, I noticed most of the tail-enders had had the good sense to shower and change. Not Gleeson however - he was dozing in a corner.

In the Test before, at Old Trafford, he had played well in a partnership of 104 with Marsh, so I said, 'Quick, Cho, shove 'em on, you're in if a wicket falls.' No sooner said than done. Not the padding up, but the wicket falling. In the time it had taken Gleeson to buckle the first strap on his left pad, Edwards was dismissed.

Marsh grabbed his bat and was halfway out the door, when I yelled out, 'Come back here, you silly bastard.'

'What do you mean, come back? Someone has to go to the crease,' growled Rod.

'Correct, Rodney, but it will be Gleeson, not you,' I replied.

Casting an eye in Cho's direction and seeing his state of undress, Rodney mused, 'The pubs will be closed by the time he's ready.'

We managed to restrain the eager 'keeper and, after what seemed like ages, Gleeson was finally on his way. At his leisurely pace the stroll to the centre took at least three minutes.

The Englishmen were incensed at what they thought were delaying tactics. The umpires were fidgety, fearing reprisal for allowing this to occur at a vital stage of the game.

Gleeson sauntered serenely past umpire Constant's wagging finger, winked reassuringly at Greg Chappell and walked to the Nursery end crease to face his first ball.

David Constant stood rigidly behind the stumps at the Pavilion end, eager to allow the angry English captain to get on with his job.

Gleeson turned slowly at the crease, glancing casually around the field, and faced up.

'Don't you want guard?' pleaded Constant.

'Don't need it,' drawled Gleeson, 'I've batted here before.'

PLAYING AT LORD'S
Christopher Martin-Jenkins

It may seem immodest of me as a player of little note, who barely reached county second eleven standard, to record for this book a personal memory of playing at Lord's rather than watching there. After all, I have played there only twice, whereas I calculate that I must have spent somewhere between six months and a year of the last fifteen years just commentating and reporting on big matches at Lord's.

This, of course, is half the problem when it comes to trying to sort out memories of years of Test matches and one-day finals of one kind and another. Besides, all are well documented, whereas my own little dramas merited only a paragraph in *Wisden* and daily reports, soon forgotten, in *The Times* and the *Telegraph*. Though I was lucky enough to be at school at a time when two-day schools matches were still played at Lord's, and when at least two of the Fleet Street newspapers sent reporters along to watch.

I had set my heart on playing for Marlborough against Rugby at Lord's from the moment I first watched the game as a small prep-school boy. It was my first experience of Lord's and I was inspired by it instantly. That grand pavilion beckoned me like a castle in the sky and the players of Rugby, in their blue shirts, and of Marlborough, the school for which I was bound, seemed virtually indistinguishable to me from Test players.

When I got to Marlborough my aim remained directly centred on Lord's. I longed for the announcement on the main school notice-board, not, as in other schools, that I had been awarded my colours, but that I had been 'invited to play at Lord's', which meant the same, yet so much more.

Having been the 'star' on my little prep school side, I had played in the requisite under-fifteen and under-sixteen school teams, but the better players of my year's intake had to wait a season longer than normal for promotion to the first eleven because of an exceptional side at the top of the school in 1961 – Mike Griffith scored over 1,000 runs and captained an unbeaten team, of which two got blues; one, Jack Hopper, would have done had he been bright enough (he became a professional golfer instead) and another, David Jones, played with success for Buckinghamshire for several years.

At last, the following season, I got my precious invitation, from J.R.W. Harvey, later a double blue at cricket and rugger, and I walked on cloud nine throughout the drawn two-day match at Lord's, making 56 and 40 and picking up a wicket or two as well. From the breakfast in the morning at the Portland Arms, round the corner from Lord's, to the drinks after the match, I treasure the whole experience. Incidently, the delightful old Portland Arms has now become a pizza house under the incredible title of 'The Third Mrs Gioconda'!

When I went back to Lord's in 1963, it was as the proud captain, and I look back on what happened with a mixture of the same pride tinged with shame and disappointment.

At first, I was relieved just to be playing, having broken a finger fielding and missed the last three matches before Lord's. I had just one net on the day before the match and fortunately felt little pain, although I had to leave out a good friend which, in a different way, was painful.

We began the match marvellously. I had been sorry to lose the toss on a dusty pitch which did not look as though it would get easier as the game progressed, but we bowled Rugby out for 99 by lunch. We ourselves managed only 135, and I was bowled for 16 by an off-break which kept very low.

Rugby then recovered well to total 233 and we began our second innings after lunch on the second day, needing 199 to win. We made a poor start but after going in at number four, I was lucky to find my form and confidence, and from 56 for four, a boy called Tim Halford, son of a Wightman Cup tennis player, and myself pushed the total to 145.

Halford was out after tea for 37, but Rugby continued to bowl me the occasional half-volley and I even managed to hit successive balls from their off-spinner into the old Tavern for sixes. The crowds for these games in those days were not inconsiderable and there was much excitement as it began to look as though Marlborough would win. A boy's dream was about, it seemed, to come true. And at Lord's!

I could imagine the tension and pride which my parents and the other members of my family must be feeling. Later I was to wish the scoreboard had not been recording the scores of the individual batsmen, merely the side's total, for the triumph of a personal century temporarily eclipsed the more important team target of 199 and I called my partner, a close friend, for a sharpish single to mid-wicket. He hesitated, the fielder's throw hit the stumps directly, and a precious wicket had gone.

I told myself not to press for my 100 now. A maiden over passed. Rugby rightly made the most of the extra tension which inevitably comes when a batsman is on 99. At last I judged that a single to cover was feasible. Again, a freak throw hit the stumps directly. This time there was a strong feeling amongst spectators that my partner had made his ground and that my 100th run had been scored. The umpire decreed otherwise.

To an inexperienced cricketer, this was too much. Still on

99, I was lucky not to be given out lbw; the other umpire, Len Muncer, was no doubt as eager as I was to see me reach a hundred! A few balls later, our number nine batsman was caught and bowled for nought.

At the other end, with 23 runs still needed for victory, I was rapped painfully on the thumb by a ball which lifted, and limply I skied the next ball to mid-on.

Instead of the walk up the pavilion steps with the bat high and victory assured, I had to face the sympathetic comments of the members in the Long Room. The tide had turned for the last time in a game of classic fluctuations, our last wicket quickly fell and the dream had suddenly died.

The saddest moment came when I walked into the Rugby dressing-room, the one occupied at home matches by Middlesex and England, to congratulate our somewhat fortunate conquerors. The contrast between their unalloyed joy and the dejection in the dressing-room I had just left was shattering. How many thousands of other cricketers in games of far more importance have known that elation or despair after a match at Lord's. There was never a ground, and certainly never a game, for so raising hopes and dashing them again. And for me there would be no further chance. At least I played there, and made some runs; and, in a curious way, to make 99 was more likely to etch the occasion on my memory than to score a hundred. I suppose that is some consolation.

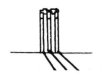

FIELDING AT SHORT LEG
Peter Walker

The element of chance plays just as important a role in cricket as in any other game. There's a limit to how much one can plan a career, and the way I ended up at short leg for Glamorgan and England is a good example of this.

In my first season as a pro I played under the captaincy of the legendary Wilfred Wooller, a man of many words and equally controversial actions. We were playing at the old Cardiff Arms Park against Warwickshire, and after winning the toss and putting them in on a blistering hot day, Wilf had reached exploding point by mid-afternoon when the opposition's score stood at 372 for two. Our captain had, as usual, opened the bowling, and at five o'clock he decided at last to make a bowling change at his end!

As very much the 'junior pro', it was my job to fill all the long distance throwing positions, so I'd spent the afternoon running from third man to third man between overs and was well shagged out by late afternoon. Passing Wilf as he stood perspiring in the middle of the pitch, I innocently enquired, as any dutiful youngster would, 'Where would you like me to go, Skipper?' The reply, suitably bowdlerised was: 'For Christ's sake, Peter, spit in the air and go where it lands!'

At eighteen years of age, if Wilf Wooller told you to spit in the air and go where it lands, you did just that. It fell at short square leg. By this time, Wilf had turned away and forgotten me. Our off-spinner, Jimmy McConnon, bowled; Alan Townsend pushed one hard off his legs, I dived to my right and caught it, and so condemned myself to sixteen years and some 700 odd catches in that position.

On such flimsy 'droppings' a career was built.

PRESS COVERAGE
Colin Milburn

I've got a little bit of advice for aspiring Test players - open the newspapers with care.

I remember keenly anticipating my Test debut at Old Trafford in 1966 against West Indies. There I was, reporting for duty the night before the game, and on my best behaviour. Not for me the normal ten-pints ritual on the eve of a match. No, being a good lad, I restricted myself to a few glasses of wine, interspersed with some cordial chat with the selectors and the rest of the players. I was even in bed early, but I don't think I slept a wink.

Never mind, into battle with the Windies and we were forced to field. On I strolled into my specialist position of forward short leg, where I had made quite an impression with Northants. Jeff Jones came steaming into bowl at Conrad Hunte, who got a little inside edge. I dived to my right but couldn't get a hand to it. All the lads said, 'Well done, hard luck'.

A bit later and the same thing happened. This time the ball flew even harder but somehow I just managed to get a finger on it, although unable to catch it. Again the lads were quite impressed by my attempt, echoing 'Well tried'. Hunte moved on to hit a century and I thought nothing more about it until I picked up one of the newspapers next morning.

Looking at the match report I noticed that in reference to Conrad Hunte it said that he had been dropped three times. Well I recalled that Ken Higgs had missed him in the outfield but, blow me, when had he been dropped three times.

Read on, Ollie old boy - yes, it was down to me according to this particular scribe. The writer observed: 'There was one thing that worried me about Milburn's selection and that was his fielding.' Charming.

Later that day I opened with Eric Russell of Middlesex against the fury of Wes Hall and Charlie Griffith. I was anxious to get off the mark. I nicked one onto the pad and it spurted into the covers. I was on my way only to see Eric suddenly sending me back. By then I was halfway down the wicket and it was a bit like asking the *QE2* to turn around on a sixpence.

My admiring cricket writer then observed in his next despatch: 'I was rather concerned about Milburn's running between the wickets when he was selected.'

Well, never mind, on to Saturday and a full house. I admit to having a bit of luck, being dropped two or three times, but even so I was quite proud to have rattled up 94.

I went back to Northampton on the rest day and could hardly wait to pick up the Sunday newspapers. Most of them were okay, but one of them - crikey, it's enough to turn you to drink! He admitted that I had made up for my first-innings duck (very good of him) but then added: 'Milburn had so much luck that if he had fallen in the Manchester Ship Canal he would have come out smelling of Chanel No 5.'

Happily to say, my relationship with the Press got easier after this introduction. In fact, they had a chuckle at my expense on more than one occasion. I recall the next Test I played against West Indies at Lord's.

I opened this time with Geoff Boycott and we soon had the Windies in trouble. They were buckling at something like 90 for five when the great Garry Sobers came in to join his cousin David Holford. They turned the game, with Holford grabbing a century and Garry racing past his own 100 in spectacular style. The West Indian fans celebrated in typical fashion by lifting Garry into the air on the pitch - a great sight.

In the England innings, I managed to hit a century and six guys came pounding onto the pitch determined to give me the Sobers' treatment. They tried to lift me but my 18-stone frame was going nowhere. I just couldn't get airborne.

One of the lads instead offered me the pint of Guinness he had brought with him. I was parched and my normal reaction would have been to down it. But I suddenly thought: hey, this is Lord's, old boy. Everyone was watching. I think it's the first drink I've ever turned down.

In the back of my mind was that my favourite cricket writer would be watching my every move. If I had drunk the Guinness

I can see it now - 'I was worried when Milburn was selected that he was a drunkard.' Well sometimes we can prove the Press wrong. . .

CLOSEY WAS SPEECHLESS
Clive Radley

Touring with Brian Close as captain was an education in itself. My first experience of this was on Derrick Robins' trip to South Africa in 1975.

We started the tour in Port Elizabeth playing Eastern Province. There was nothing too unusual about the game: we scored about 350, they got a similar total and in the second innings we managed another high score on what was still an extremely good wicket.

Brian decided the wicket was still so good that we couldn't afford to give them any chance. He maintained there was only one winner and we could never hope to bowl them out on such a flat strip, so he just made a token declaration and set an impossible target of 360 in just over three hours.

We hadn't banked on a chap called Graeme Pollock, who played what I still consider the best knock I have ever seen, scoring 150 in as many minutes and leading Eastern Province to victory with about five overs to spare.

Closey was absolutely livid (there were not many worse losers than him). He slammed the dressing-room door shut and shouted, 'We're not having any press, any opposition in here until we've sat down and analysed what happened out there!'

He started off with what seemed to be a monumental team rocket by saying, 'Now, have any of you youngsters learnt anything by what happened out there?' Sitting next to me was a young chap called John Lyon, a wicket-keeper and understudy to Farokh Engineer at Old Trafford. He hadn't said anything on the tour so far and we had been there a week, but when Closey said 'Have any of you youngsters learnt anything?', he put up his hand and said: 'Yes, Mr Close, I've learnt something - you declared too bloody early, that's what I've learnt.'

Closey, for a change, was speechless!

A MEMORABLE TEST MATCH
Sir Donald Bradman

I am charged with the job of writing a cricket story for The Lord's Taverners' book and am taking as my theme the second Test at Lord's between Australia and England in 1930. I do so because I think this was a magnificent match in which all the facets of the game were on display in a manner befitting the finest traditions of Test cricket.

Both sides had beautifully balanced selections. England's team was a captain's dream in that it contained a fast bowler to open one end (Allen) plus a medium-fast the other end (Tate), supported by a left-hand first-finger spinner (White) and a right-hand, leg-spin googly bowler (Robins). The reserve attack was another right-hand medium-pacer (Hammond) and a second left-hand first-finger spinner (Woolley).

Australia had a fast bowler (Wall) supported by two medium-pacers (Fairfax and McCabe), with the leg-spinner (Grimmett) and a left-hand first-finger spinner (Hornibrook) as the old ball brigade.

In batting, England had left- and right-hand openers (Hobbs and Woolley), plus a strong line-up to follow which included another left-hander (Chapman). Australia did not possess quite the same variety because she had no top line left-hand batsman.

The match was played in beautiful weather on a pitch which

encouraged batsmen to play their shots freely. England won the toss and at the end of the first day had accumulated 405 for nine. As the match was limited to four days, some commentators believed Chapman could have closed at that figure, but he elected to bat on until the side was all out for 425.

The outstanding feature of England's batting was a glorious century by Duleepsinhji, playing in his first Test. The young Indian played with a lissom grace that charmed friend and foe alike. His strokes were deceptively powerful. I had the job of fielding in the covers when Grimmett was bowling and my hands were sore from stopping his drives.

In the finish I caught him almost on the boundary at extra cover from a lofted drive. His total of 173 took four and three-quarter hours and must have pleased the great Ranji who, I understand, watched the whole innings. Rumour has it that Ranji gently rebuked him for getting out off a careless shot.

When Woodfull and Ponsford opened for Australia it was generally felt that Australia would be on the defensive, but these two solid openers put together a partnership of 162, of which Ponsford made exactly half. In accordance with accepted custom the players were presented to His Majesty the King around the time of the tea interval. Immediately following that break in the play Ponsford was caught at slip, causing some pressmen to say England's best bowler that afternoon was the King.

I was next in and recall clearly that my first delivery was from Jack White, a ball to which I jumped down the pitch and drove into the covers. Woodfull was eventually out ten minutes before close of play on the second day having made 155, and by a coincidence I was 155 not out at stumps.

On the Monday, Australia continued piling on the runs at great speed and finally Woodfull closed the innings at 729 for six wickets. There was temporary confusion when the scoreboard couldn't produce the requisite 7. My own innings ended when I was on 254. It was without doubt the most technically satisfying of my career. I batted altogether 330 minutes and in the whole of the innings only played two strokes which did not go precisely where I intended them to.

The first was a defensive stroke to which I got a thick edge towards second slip, and the second was a cover drive from which I was dismissed. Actually the latter went almost exactly where I intended it to go but I lofted the ball just enough for Percy Chapman to grab it in his outstretched right hand (he was a natural left-hander), inches from the ground. The ball was travelling like a rocket and I believe it was the finest catch ever to dismiss me in my whole career.

In England's second innings her outstanding batsman was Chapman, who played a breezy swashbuckling knock for 121 in which he really gave Clarrie Grimmett the stick. Percy took chances and led a charmed existence. Early on he skied a simple catch to cover but Ponsford and Richardson both left it to the other, only to see the catch fall harmlessly to earth.

Finally England totalled 375, thus leaving Australia a mere 72 to win. It looked a foregone conclusion as there was plenty of time, but amidst great tension and excitement Australia lost three wickets (including mine) for 22 runs. This time I was caught by Chapman, fielding in the gully, who picked up off his shoe laces a powerfully struck cut - another really wonderful piece of fielding. Suddenly England seemed to be in with a chance, but Woodfull and McCabe steered Australia safely home with about one and a half hours left for play.

The match produced magnificent batting by both sides, brilliant fielding, and even though the bowling figures suffered from the batting onslaught, there was much to admire and a great variety to savour. In ninety minutes less than the full four days allotted to the match no less than 1,601 runs had been scored, so that was a scoring rate of roughly 400 runs per day.

Australia bowled 244.8 overs, England 260.2, so that 505 overs were sent down at the rate of approximately 132 per day; or close to 24 per hour. Looking at the quality and balance of the bowling sides, it makes a mockery of the funereal rates served up by most modern sides where there is undue reliance on fast and medium-pace bowlers who take run-ups out of all proportion to their speed.

I have seen more exciting, more intense struggles, but from an enjoyment point of view I think that wonderful Lord's Test produced everything spectators could ask for. It will always live in my memory.

SIDE BET
Godfrey Evans

In 1953, playing against our old adversaries Australia, we won the Ashes for the first time since the infamous Bodyline tour of 1932-33. Our captain, Len Hutton, led us to victory in the fifth Test at the Oval.

I remember it well: Denis Compton sweeping the ball to the leg boundary off the bowling of Arthur Morris, to score the winning runs. A keen cricket enthusiast rushed up to Denis and gave him £100. 'I'll double it if you do the same in Australia,' the man said.

In the winter of 1954-55 we went to Australia to defend the Ashes. We lost the first Test at Brisbane, won the second at Sydney, and the third at Melbourne. A victory at Adelaide would give us the series and ensure that we kept the Ashes. England were in the box seat and wanted just 94 in the last innings to win. Keith Miller had us struggling, capturing the first three wickets for 18 runs. Trevor Bailey and Denis Compton were taking the score nearer and nearer the winning total, then Trevor was out with six runs to go.

I was next in. My first ball we scampered a leg bye. This gave me the bowling, with Keith Miller still trying like mad. We took two to third man; the next was an horrific bouncer I just managed to avoid. The third ball, well up on the leg stump, I whacked for four. We had won the series and retained the Ashes, to cheers from the dressing-room.

As we came off the field, Denis said: 'You bloody fool, Godders! What did you want to do that for?'

'To win the series!' I said excitedly.

'If you had let me hit that winning run, I would have won £200,' said Denis.

'Why didn't you tell me, we could have shared it.'

'I didn't want to put you off,' came his reply, smiling all over his face.

Denis was really thinking of the party he could have had with £200. As it was, he said, 'Well done, Godders'. We had a hell of a party anyway.

A GOOD SOAK
Pat Pocock

My first season coincided with Ken Barrington's benefit year, and, quite naturally, he had worked hard to make the haul as large and as lucrative as possible. He had arranged no fewer than twenty Sunday games, one for every weekend of the season. I played in one of these games at Aldermaston, where, on the hottest day of the year, I opened the batting with Stuart Surridge, captain of Surrey's famous team of the fifties. I stayed around for half an hour, scored a few runs, and came off the field with my shirt dripping with sweat. As I started to search for the showers, I met Ron Tindall, who was awaiting his turn to bat.

'Sorry, Perce,' he said. 'It's only a small ground and there's no showers. But don't worry, they've made arrangements for us to wash in that house over there. Don't go in the front door, use the side door.'

So I picked up my sponge bag and towel, walked down the road to the house and found the room which Ron had described. Unfortunately there was no shower, so I ran a deep bath and lay there, singing and soaking. Suddenly a stranger put his head round the door. I was slightly surprised that he hadn't knocked before entering, but then, it was his house and gratitude was in order.

'Hello,' I said. 'The lads told me about the arrangement. Very kind of you.' He didn't seem able to speak. He spluttered quite a lot and shook his head a few times, then he disappeared. I finished my bath and my song, considered borrowing my host's aftershave and strolled back to the cricket ground, impeccably groomed for the evening's entertainment. The first person I met was Ron.

'Thank you very much,' I said, 'I really needed that bath.'

He almost dropped his pint. 'Oh no,' he said. 'You didn't take me seriously? You didn't really go to a strange house and jump into the bath? Suppose his wife had walked in? Suppose he'd called the police? You must have known I was pulling your leg.'

I often wonder if that hospitable stranger has a good memory for faces!

SPOTTING TALENT
M.J.K. Smith

Anyone who has sat for any length of time on a County Committee will have plenty of experience of outstanding young players who faded away, or left and blossomed elsewhere. There are some real horror stories here. Essex had first chance for both Tich Freeman and Jack Hobbs, Warwickshire, Wilfred Rhodes, Hedley Verity and Bill Bowes, and of current players, Neal Radford was released by Lancashire, and Glamorgan's outstanding young batsman Matthew Maynard spent two years on the Kent staff.

Someone gets the blame, usually the coach and the Cricket Committee, but what a difficult task it can be, even to get the first part right - what is he best at? Take this England team:

Alan Oakman	Sussex
Raman Subba Row	Northants
Ken Barrington	Surrey
Maurice Tremlett	Somerset
Ian Botham	Worcester
Godfrey Evans	Kent
Derek Underwood	Kent
Don Shepherd	Glamorgan
Tom Cartwright	Warwickshire
Harold Rhodes	Derby
Derek Shackleton	Hampshire

Alan Oakman joined Sussex as an off-spinner, but found his way blocked by Robin Marlar and so had to concentrate on his batting. Raman Subba Row I remember first bowling very slow leg-breaks for Cambridge in the Varsity Match and batting well down the order. He too was pushed into opening and finished up making all the major overseas tours. Ken Barrington was another young leg-spinner when he joined Surrey and became, for many, England's best post-war number three. Immediately after the war there were no young fast bowlers and the first great white hope was Maurice Tremlett, who made headlines in 1947 in his debut game for Somerset against Middlesex at Lord's, with Edrich and Compton in the opposition, by taking 8 for 86 in the game. That winter he toured the West Indies and then went to South Africa the following year. He lost his bowling completely, but then had a long and successful career in the middle order. Ian Botham to bat number five. I gather there is a report on him as a youngster that... 'he usually catches them - if he gets there; he can't bowl and is just a slogger with the bat.' It is perhaps kinder not to mention who wrote the report.

I was thinking recently how difficult it is for anyone trying to follow him in the Test team, since the inevitable comparisons will be made. Should Derek Pringle, Phillip DeFreitas, David Capel or any other, achieve a Test career record of, say, 175 wickets, 50 catches and 2,500 runs, he would be rated in the highest class. Yet these figures are just 50 per cent of Botham's, with presumably more to come.

We are well set up for wicket-keepers. Godfrey Evans joined Kent as a batsman as did Les Ames before him, while Arthur McIntyre joined Surrey as another young leg-spinner. But probably the most unusual turn around here was John Gleeson: an up-country club 'keeper in Australia who foiled them in the nets with his very unorthodox back-of-the-hand spin, so he took off the gloves and very quickly made the Australian XI.

We don't produce many slow left-handers now. Derek Underwood just about answers the criteria, since when he first played for Kent he bowled over the wicket and was basically a seamer. It was two or three seasons working it all out before he decided to stay round the wicket and concentrate on spinners. Ian Folley of Lancashire was outstandingly the most successful left-arm spinner in County cricket in 1987. He made a greater change than Derek, since as an opening bowler he was considerably quicker and as spinner much slower.

Off-spinners there are a plenty. I have selected Don Shepherd since he was so successful with over 2,000 wickets, but was not capped. He first opened the bowling for Glamorgan as a swing bowler. Fred Titmus bowled seamers in his early years at Middlesex and Eddie Hemmings played first for Warwickshire as a medium-pacer. At under-16 level for Warwickshire bowling off-spinners was Gladstone Small, complete with glasses. The story goes that in a Club match someone bowled a couple round his ears and he went on a long run to sort the matter out, and very quickly on to the Warwick staff. The glasses kept falling off in his delivery, so when last he trod on them, they were never replaced.

Three seamers to complete the side. Harold Rhodes, the quickest, bowled leg-spinners like his father Dusty, who also played for Derbyshire and who I believe did it the other way round by changing from pace to spin. Then Derek Shackleton and Tom Cartwright, who both started as batsmen. Tom went in first for Warwickshire, aged 17, and at one stage was reluctant to play other than as an opening batsman. In a

Second Eleven Championship play-off against Yorkshire at Scarborough, Tom Dollery put him on for one over to change his bowlers round. He took a wicket, stayed on and finished with 7 for 19 from 26 overs. From that time his bowling gradually took over.

Few batsmen of that period could think of anything worse than having him at one end and Derek Shackleton at the other. No-one hit the seam more often than these two. Shack was reckoned to bowl a couple of looseners in April and that was it for the season. Unremitting accuracy in line and length typified their method and, with Underwood and Shepherd to follow, the fielding captain could just about go on his holidays. He certainly wouldn't be leaving many problems behind.

I thought about slipping Garry Sobers in the middle order but decided that was a little unfair. Although he first got into the Barbados side as a slow left-armer, and also the West Indies XI, it is hard to imagine he didn't always promise runs, and in fact he went in first against Australia as an 18-year-old. I remember his reply when asked who coached him: 'Oh, we just watched Frank' - Frank Worrell. Even in a nightmare, no coach could have missed his ability. It is interesting, though, that as a bowler he was most successful bowling quick, and before taking up this style he had played Test cricket bowling both slow left-hand orthodox and back-of-the-hand.

Lance Gibbs the most successful of Test-match spinners also changed his style. He told me he played in a Guyana trial match and was given so much stick by Robert Christiani, who was a fine batsman over here on the 1950 tour, overshadowed by the three Ws, that he decided there had to be a better way and took up off-spinning.

So don't shoot the coach if your man has not made it - perhaps his real strength is football.

28

REFLECTED GLORY
Alan Oakman

Gubby Allen, who was Chairman of the Selectors, phoned the Hastings police and said: 'Do you know where Alan Oakman lives?' The reply was, 'We do, and if he is in town we will pick him up in five minutes.' Four minutes later there was a knock on my door. When I opened it, a policeman, leaning on his bicycle, told me I had to report to Old Trafford the following morning. It was July 1956.

On the morning of the match there were twelve players, but I was told by captain Peter May that I had been included in the eleven. England won the toss and Peter Richardson and Colin Cowdrey never looked in any trouble during an opening stand of 174. The Reverend David Sheppard and Peter May carried on where the openers had left off, and on the Friday Godfrey Evans hit a cyclonic 47 in 29 minutes to enable England to reach the total of 459 runs.

McDonald and Burke opened the innings for Australia with a stand of 48. When Lock and Laker were brought on, the batsmen began to find things difficult. Tony Lock took the first wicket, and from that moment onwards Jim Laker took over.

At the time I was fielding at mid-on, a position to which I was unaccustomed - when playing for Sussex I had always been at slip. David Sheppard had come out of retirement and was fielding in the bat and pad position for Jim, and after a few overs went up to Peter May and said: 'As I haven't played County Cricket for a year or so and my reflexes aren't what they used to be, could I go to mid-on or mid-off and have more time to see the ball?' This was being said by a very modest man as he had scored 113 against Miller and Lindwall. Peter May promptly turned to me and said: 'Would you mind doing it?' I agreed as I was used to fielding there for the Sussex off-spinner Robin Marlar.

Having the greatest confidence in Jim as an accurate spin bowler, I stood nearer than normal. I can remember Keith

Miller coming in, taking guard and looking round the field, particularly out to deep square leg and mid-wicket. Whilst he was doing this, and not looking at me, he said, 'That's a dangerous position, Oakie. If I middle one, they will have to carry you off.' Three balls later he pushed forward and I caught one low down round my ankles - exit Miller. Jim continued to spin right through the Australian tail and they were all out for 84; 375 behind. Jim Laker 9 for 37.

On Saturday the weather took over and there was only three-quarters of an hour's play. Monday was nearly as bad. At close of play Australia were 84 for no wicket. Overnight, the weather had improved and play began ten minutes late. Due to more determined and resolute batting by the Australians, the score was 114 for two with four hours left.

After lunch the sun appeared and the ball began to turn and lift on the drying pitch. Here were the two best spin bowlers to exploit a situation like this; but it was Laker who took the advantage, although Tony never gave in.

Even when Jim was coming up to his fourteenth wicket, Lockie was still trying and getting more and more annoyed with himself because he knew under these conditions that he and Jim should have shared the wickets. Although he bowled well, and repeatedly beat the bat, he never had a catch dropped or a stumping missed. When Jim had Maddocks lbw to finish the match, we could hardly believe he had taken nineteen wickets.

The Lock and Laker of the modern cricket world would be Derek Underwood and John Emburey. Could you imagine Derek taking the first wicket in a Test match and John the remaining nineteen, under the same conditions?

Later that year, I went to a dinner with Jim Laker and he was introduced as the man who had taken nineteen wickets in the Old Trafford Test. I was then introduced as the man who had helped Jim by holding five catches. While this was going on Jim whispered in my ear, 'You're not still living on that?' It is now thirty-two years later and I am still.

VINTAGE LAKER
Peter West

Two tales of dear old Jim Laker, of whom I was very fond. He had a remarkable gift for bringing an anecdote to mind about almost every match in which he had played.

He always recalled with wry pleasure a question put to him by a young press reporter (no names, no pack drill) following his astonishing bowling analysis (eight wickets for 2 runs) in the 1950 Test trial at Bradford. 'Would that,' the enquiring journalist asked, 'have been your best performance?'

That was the season of the three Ws - Weekes, Worrell and Walcott - and of Ramadhin and Valentine. Everton de Courcy Weekes was arguably the greatest of that batting triumvirate. Jim Laker asked him one day why he had been christened Everton. 'Well,' Weekes explained, 'my dad was a soccer nut and when I arrived on the scene, Everton won the championship.'

'Really?' said James. 'A bloody good job it wasn't West Bromwich Albion!'

THE COSMO CLUB
Frank Tyson

One of my friends thought, erroneously, that the 'Cosmos' were an elite multi-national soccer team which played in America during the 1970s. Another - a real 'telly' addict - mistakenly believed Cosmo was the long-suffering, bungling lawyer-comedian in the *Topper* series on the box in the 1950s. Yet another - a rare and more erudite member of my inner circle of acquaintances - looked up the word in the dictionary, and came up with the solution that Cosmos meant the world or universe as an ordered system.

In fact this last 'clever clogs' was very close to the mark. The real, honest-to-God Cosmos were a harmonious human organisation: a social club formed within the Northamptonshire County Cricket Club ground staff by wicket-keeper Keith Andrew and I in the late fifties.

Looking back on those days, I suppose it would be less than honest not to admit that, whilst the Cosmos were a fun mob, the concept was fairly puerile. The club met on the first night of every Northants away game under a chairman nominated by his immediate predecessor. Attendance was compulsory, even for the 'Mr Glums' of the side. Shop talk was forbidden, no swearing allowed and the convivial drinks, taken in moderation I need not add, over a maximum of an hour, had to be consumed left-handed. Facetious toasts were proposed to 'Wives and Sweethearts, may they never meet' and there was the usual injection of profane songs such as 'The Wild West Show'. You know the sort of thing:

(Chorus)   Oh we're off to see the Wild West Show
              The elephant and the kangaroo
              Never mind the weather,
              So long as we're together.
              We're off to see the Wild West Show

(Individual) *(Recitative)* And now ladies and gentlemen
              We have the Oooh-Aaah Bird.

(Chorus)   The Oooh-Aaah Bird?

(Individual) *(Recitative)* Yes, the Oooh-Aaah Bird.
              This bird lays a very large square egg from a
              very small anal orifice.
              Hence its call and its name:
              Oooh-Aaah!

The club struck its own tie: a dark blue cravat with a silver weather-vane motif and the motto below: *Essayez toujours*

- always try. There was even a 'Ram's Tie' - in actual fact it was the tie of the Queenstown Woolgrowers' Association of South Africa, with an enormous ram's head in argent embroidered on an azure field. Each meeting, the Ram's Tie was awarded, on the evidence of some laughing Judas within the side, to the team member who had enjoyed the most titillating and fictional off-field experience since our last get-together.

Violations of the Cosmos' regulations were inevitably brought to the chairman's attention at each meeting by some 'super-grass' and always incurred a savage fine of a bob or two. In the true tradition of British justice, the accused could always appeal to the higher court of the chairman and two of his nominated cronies. But since such a tactic rarely resulted in anything but the doubling of the original fine, the wiser course of action was to accept the umpire's initial decision.

It was all so childish - yet it was all so successful in contributing to the *esprit de corps* which brought Northamptonshire a modicum of success in the late 1950s. Ten years earlier the industrial paternalism of the tapered-roller bearing company of British Timpken and its cricket-loving chairman of directors, Sir John Pascoe, had initiated a head-hunting drive for cricketing talent which brought a plethora of playing ability flocking to the small Midland county: men of the ilk of Surrey's Freddie Brown and Lancashire's Albert Nutter and Norman Oldfield who played for Northants during the summer and worked for British Timpken in the winter months. Northamptonshire acquired the nickname of 'Timpkenshire' and spread its recruitment net so wide that it scooped up not only inexplicable rejects from other English counties but also batsmen and bowlers from overseas, all seeking opportunities in the first-class game.

In the space of less than a decade Northants had summoned to its colours Yorkshiremen of the ability of Des Barrick, Fred Jakeman, Ken Fiddling and Doug Greasley. They joined fellow Tyke and opener Dennis Brookes, who had been a fixture at the Wantage Road Ground since 1934. From Lancashire came blinking 'Buddy' Oldfield - another number one batsman who, but for the Second World War and a nervous temperament, must surely have played more than his one Test for England. Other 'Lankies' included Bert Nutter, Vince Broderick, Syd Starkie, nonpareil wicket-keeper Keith Andrew, and one of England's fastest post-war bowlers, Frank Tyson.

Nor were Commonwealth countries neglected. Australia contributed to the Northants cause in the persons of the number three, double century specialist, 'Jock' Livingston, the left-handed over-the-wrist spinner George Tribe - who performed the 'double' in seven of eight summers with his adopted county - and the orthodox 'molly-duke' spinner, Jack Manning, who three times surpassed the hundred-wicket milestone in a season.

Quite often sharing the responsibility of going in first with Dennis Brookes in the fifties was the phlegmatic Kiwi, Peter Arnold, whose solid style contrasted starkly in efficiency and sturdiness with that of fellow New Zealander, Test representative, John Guy: a passing comet on the Northants horizon in 1958.

Trinidadian middle-order batsman Donald Ramsamooj flattered the Midland county for a while with his flamboyance, only to deceive with his lack of consistency. Springbok and Oxford all-rounder, 'Pom-Pom' Fellows-Smith, on the other hand, gave the appearance of solidity in his one season with Northants but revealed little of the form which was to win him a South African cap in 1960.

Closer to home, the minor counties of Shropshire and Bedfordshire sent their likely lads to the Northamptonshire standard in the persons of all-rounders Albert Lightfoot and the two Watts brothers, Peter and Jim. When England batsman-to-be Raman Subba Row and his Surrey colleague, medium-pacer Harry Kelleher, directed their steps towards Cobbler Town in 1955 and 1956 respectively, they left places for only two local players - 'Nobby' Clarke and Brian Reynolds - in the Northants team. It had become a polyglot League of Nations side and there were strong rumours around the county circuit that its next recruit would be an Eskimo!

Whilst the Midland county had built up a formidable Ministry of Cricketing Talents, it was a cabinet based on individual professionalism rather than the loyalty that Lancastrians and Yorkshiremen feel towards a place and a habitation. In some respects, the Northants Cosmo Club provided the essential super-glue of team spirit to the Wantage Road ground: the cement which in other teams was a collective birthright.

For the Cosmos was not a boozing club. It organised togetherness, especially on Sunday, our one free day of the week. If we were playing at Taunton near the seaside, a spin down to Torquay to bathe our aching feet in the briny was the order of the day. If we were inland, impromptu golf tourneys based on bizarre handicapping were mounted.

Our collectiveness extended to pre-match and post-game activities. At Worcester, keeper 'K.V.' Andrew organised a costly early morning chipping competition, to discover who could lob a golf ball with a seven iron across the River Severn from a tee on the lawn of our riverside hotel. Once, in the north of England, the same stumper instigated an hilarious evening group visit to an annual 'wakes' fair on the first evening of a three-day game. He won a goldfish at a side-show and kept it in his hotel bath for the remaining two days of the match - much to the consternation of the housemaids - before transporting it home in a plastic bag filled with water.

Practical jokes were everyday occurrences amongst the Cosmopolitans. Three members who missed a Saturday evening Abergavenny meeting to play in a benefit game on the following day, returned at one o'clock on Monday morning - to find their hotel room denuded of every stick of furniture, including the beds. Another pair of miscreants actually 'lost' their Worcester hotel room. Whilst they were playing truant from a plenary session, a large wardrobe was moved from its original hallway position and placed over the doorway to the chamber into which they had earlier moved their luggage. The entrance to room number 14 simply ceased to exist and it required an enquiry at the reception desk to determine whither it had disappeared!

The zenith of the Cosmo era, however, was, in the language of James Thurber, The Day of the Great Fishing Trip. Northants were playing Sussex in a southern coastal resort and it was decided that the Cosmos would preface what threatened to be a rather uninteresting final day's play with an early morning sea-fishing expedition. On the eve of the great event, the twelfth man was despatched to purchase the appropriate quantities of handlines, paternosters and bait. It was still early summer and when the fractious band of cricketing Isaac Waltons were rousted from their beds at 5am and frogmarched to the local pier, dawn had not yet broken. We stumbled over the entrance turnstiles, since the pier was not yet opened, made our way to the end of the jetty and baited up blindly. Twelve lines went over the side together - and almost simultaneously came the thud of twelve weights hitting sand! The tide was out and the sea had retreated almost a mile beyond the end of the pier! The names of Keith Andrew and Frank Tyson were Brighton mud for many weeks after that fiasco in the Cosmo Camp.

Even such debacles, however, could not mar the club's annual end-of-season get-together which came to be held by tradition at the Falcon Inn at Castle Ashby, a pretty little village a few miles outside Northampton. There, for several years, Cosmos and their wives foregathered to spend the accumulated fines of the season on a hazy evening of good Phipps ale in the cellar bar, a delicious meal of succulent trout in the dining room and endless games of skittles in the bowling alley. Appositely, the Cosmos always staged the grand finale to their summer in the spirit of togetherness which for the most part had characterised Northamptonshire's on-field achievements throughout the season.

In retrospect, I am still amazed that the simplistic concept of the Northants Cosmo Club - allied admittedly to a galaxy of talent - was so successful. The Midland county finished second in the County Championship in 1957 and were seldom conclusively out of contention for the premiership, in a decade which was dominated for 70 per cent of the time by the mighty Surrey combination led by Stuart Surridge and Peter May. For me, the Cosmos proved two immutable cricketing truths: team spirit and a sense of enjoyment are a brace of essentials in every really successful cricket team.

FACING A TYPHOON
Charles Palmer

With Frank Tyson missing the first three Tests against the visiting Australians in 1956 through a leg bone fracture, and Fred Trueman doubtless still feeling he had to justify his selection against competition from the now fit Tyson and Statham, the scene was set for a battle for the selectors' favour before the fourth Test. The selectors chose Tyson and Trueman for the 150th anniversary Gentlemen v Players match at Lord's, and so they came together as opening bowlers for the first time in the season.

At the start of its match report, *Wisden*, in its impersonal detached style, states that Tyson's return to representative cricket 'was of major interest and his bowling for the Players gave satisfactory evidence of his recovery'.

The Players elected to bat first, but rain brought the day's play to an early finish with the score 216 for eight. On the second morning with the rain still about, the Players, without having the pitch rolled, finished their innings and then the Gentlemen were, says *Wisden*, 'subjected to really hostile bowling by Tyson and Trueman'. The Gentlemen's dressing-room, containing players like Peter Richardson, Doug Insole, Trevor Bailey and Robin Marlar, was never likely to suffer from oppressive silence but their repartee was far exceeded by Middlesex fast bowler John Warr who, due in at number eight, wisecracked his way throughout the efforts of the earlier batsmen against what I can certainly confirm was this 'really hostile bowling'.

Later in the innings, after a stoppage for rain, J.M. Allan and Trevor Bailey resumed strike on the rain-enlivened wicket against a Tyson still frustrated at having taken only one of the six wickets already to fall. The batsmen who were already out looked on with great interest but with the equanimity born of earlier dismissal; those still to bat watched with keen apprehension on what effect the rain had had. They did not have to wait long. In Tyson's first over from the pavilion end a shortish ball took off like a nuclear missile. Jimmy Allan at first appeared unaffected, only realising the full significance of what had happened when the ball had long gone high over his head, high over wicket-keeper Godfrey Evans' high leap, and had thudded into the sightscreen.

The shocked consensus in the dressing-room was that the ball bounced twice before hitting the sightscreen; the few yet to bat thought only once. Whether once or twice (or more) it had a profound effect on John Warr as next batsman in. His wisecracking dried up; we swore he visibly paled and after full realisation had dawned was heard to reflect pensively:

'I don't know whether to mediate, emigrate or defecate.'

Well - or some such words!

LEARNING THE HARD WAY
Peter Graves

The venue is Southampton in the mid-seventies, Sussex versus Hampshire. Sussex are captained by P.H. Graves in the absence of Tony Greig on Test duty. It's a flat wicket and Graves calls the toss incorrectly. 'Sorry, lads, we're in the field!' It is the first year of the statutory 100 overs and Sussex walk onto the field knowing that Barry Richards and Gordon Greenidge will be right behind them.

It was a pleasantly sunny sort of day, the kind of day which indicates to you from early on that you will be out there fielding throughout its entirety!

Sussex had five recognised bowlers in their line-up, and if we did not get the early breakthrough, the captain foresaw that with these five to share 100 overs it could mean a shuffle of the card pack on a regular basis that day. Hampshire got off to a comfortable start. The openers negotiated the first half hour and then began picking up runs in their own respective styles with ease. Richards got bored and got out, but not before there was close to 100 on the board. David Turner came in and started squirting the ball around, as is his fashion, straight away. By now the off-spinner, John Barclay, was wheeling away, bowling tidily but to a very defensive field.

Sussex at that time had a few youngsters in their team, talented but inexperienced, one of whom was named Simon Hoadley. This particular chap was in the side as a batsman, but as the field changed around at the end of each over he kept remarking that he could bowl as well. 'Can I have a bowl now, Skip?' he urged after every hour in his inimitable mid-Sussex brogue, like a Jack Russell snapping at one's heels. After a while his persistence got to me. I reasoned that with Greenidge on 140 and Hampshire 250 for two, we ought to try a sixth bowler anyway! And so, the scene was set: Simon Hoadley, debutant right-arm off-spinner, bowling to Greenidge.

The field was set in similar fashion to John Barclay's and the bowler, having listened to his captain about length and line and bowling to his field, marked out his run-up. He turned and bowled his first ball. It was pleasantly flighted and on the spot, too. Regrettably, however, this did not make any difference to the batsman, who took one step down the wicket and hit the ball between deep mid-off and extra cover, one bounce for four. 'Well bowled,' enthused his captain. 'Keep it there.'

The bowler did, but the next ball Greenidge despatched over the sightscreen for six. The captain encouraged his bowler, but deep down knew that however well any bowler turned his arm over, Greenidge was likely to make a mockery of ability - and anyway, apart from the bowler, we only had ten fielders!

Simon Hoadley dutifully completed his over, but not before Greenidge had pasted him for 4 6 4 6 4. To the purist, Hoadley had not bowled a bad over, but having taken his short-sleeve sweater from the umpire, he walked across to his captain and said, 'Can I come off now, Skip?' Pure pathos, I thought. The umpire did not take his sweater again in the match. Greenidge completed a personal 250, and by the end of the 100 overs Jesty and Gilliat had taken Hampshire to a grand total of 501 for five.

As the Sussex team trudged off the field, Simon Hoadley was left to reflect - but not for long, as he was soon to be batting against Andy Roberts. But that's another story.

PRACTICAL JOKER
Bob Taylor

I suppose every touring team, whether it be cricket, rugby, soccer or any other such game, needs a joker in the party to help with team spirit.

England cricket touring teams always spend upwards of two to four months away from home, living out of suitcases, moving from hotels to airports to cricket grounds. When the initial novelty has worn thin these activities can become somewhat tiresome and monotonous, not least the inevitable frustration of hanging around airport lounges waiting for your flight call etc. This is when you need someone, sometimes, to relieve the tension and boredom.

The England touring party to Australia and New Zealand in 1974-75 had such a person in David Lloyd, the former Lancashire captain. Everywhere we went in Australia he would pop into the local joke shop and buy everything from Laurel and Hardy masks and bowler hats to stink bombs and exploding cigarettes. It sounds a little childish, but performed in the right spirit, it can be quite funny.

One such occasion was when the touring party was waiting for a flight call from Melbourne to Sydney. Melbourne's Tullamarine Airport, then almost brand new, looked very bright and modern and spotlessly clean, until a certain David Lloyd produced a very realistic curly wurly dog mess and placed it on the airport lounge floor, just in front of the

England players.

The hilarity and laughter seemed to last for ages, as we watched the Australian passengers rushing for their flights, tripping over and pulling funny faces at this revolting looking object. The joke was starting to wear off, when we saw an airport attendant carrying a brush, shovel and bucket, obviously intent on cleaning up the reported mess. He was just bending down to brush it onto his shovel when David stood up, grabbed the thing and put it into his pocket. The look of amazement on this chap's face set the touring party off in hysterics. It would have been an ideal situation for television's *Candid Camera*. As it was, it gave the England lads something to laugh about.

STRONG WORDS
Alf Gover

England versus New Zealand at The Oval in 1937, with Denis Compton at the commencement of his distinguished Test career. Skipper Walter Robins, sending down his leg-spinners, is driven hard towards mid-off where Denis is fielding, but not with 100 per cent concentration on the game. He is late in his reaction and completely misses the ball, which carries on to the boundary fence. Standing at mid-on I wait for the blast from the skipper. It comes. Walter, a stickler for exemplary fielding, calls out, 'I will make it my business to see that you never play for England again.'

Years later, when Denis had become a shining star in the England Test eleven and I was cricket correspondent of the *Sunday Mirror*, I reminded Walter of his words and asked if he remembered the incident and whether he would have any objection to my using the story in my weekly column.

Walter not only had no objection but had a good laugh as he recalled the occasion. Looking back over the many great Test innings Denis played after that match, the mind boggles at what England would have lost had the threat been carried out.

TEST DEBUT
Keith Andrew

I shall always remember 25 November 1954. It was the day before the first Test match between England and Australia at Brisbane. It was the day I heard over the local radio that Godfrey Evans was ill and that I might be playing for England the following day. That night, as I lay awake in the famous Lennon's Hotel, I thought of the great players on both sides. I thought of my name being printed against theirs, cigarette card names about whom I was still starry-eyed. After all, not much more than a year before, I had been playing for my battalion side in the Army.

In the morning, the news that I was definitely playing came over the radio, later to be confirmed by the captain, Len Hutton. The fact that those in the game rated me highly when standing up to the wicket did nothing for my confidence on that November day, especially when I realised that England were going into the match without one recognised spin bowler of any type. The teams in batting order were as follows - Australia: Les Favell, Arthur Morris, Keith Miller, Neil Harvey, Graeme Hole, Richie Benaud, Ron Archer, Ray Lindwall, Gil Langley, Ian Johnson, Bill Johnston. England: Len Hutton, Reg Simpson, Bill Edrich, Denis Compton, Peter May, Colin Cowdrey, Trevor Bailey, Frank Tyson, Keith Andrew, Alec Bedser, Brian Statham.

Jim Swanton's late communiqué read: 'Evans did not recover from an attack of sunstroke and had to be replaced by Andrew. Australia left out Davidson from the twelve previously named.'

And so began my most memorable match, a five-day experience that affected my life in so many ways. It could have been a disaster, but apart from the result, it wasn't. In fact, I don't think it was for any of us, on reflection. It gave me the incentive to try to become something I wasn't at the time - a top-class wicket-keeper. More importantly, it taught me to live with pressure, even to enjoy it. It taught me that sometimes heroes have feet of clay, but it also gave me the opportunity of meeting Denis Compton and Bill Edrich, special men who understood. It seemed to teach even that most remote of men, Len Hutton, that balance is essential to any team plan, although I am sure he was the first to realise that slowing down the over rate was effective in terms of results, if of nothing else.

We won the toss and had no alternative, I suppose, but to field. Lord Hawke, another famous Yorkshireman, may not have agreed, but I quote Hutton, or Sir Leonard as he now is: 'As I have no slow bowling, my only hope of winning is to get Australia out cheaply while the wicket is new and then try for a long lead. So, with some misgivings, I am going to do what no-one but the oldest can remember a captain doing before in a Test match in Australia and put them in to bat'.

He may well have been right. We dropped a considerable number of catches, certainly double figures were reached if we count half-chances. Neither were we the fittest team in the world. Denis Compton broke a finger fielding on the first day and Alec Bedser was never well, as was proved when it was discovered that he had developed shingles. One or two of us also got a touch of the sun, but there was no getting away from the fact that 'Catches win matches'. Subsequent events proved this conclusively.

I will go on record and say that if Godfrey Evans had played, the result would have been very different. Contrary to reports at the time, I did not miss one catch throughout the match - a catch that I got a hand to, that is. In fact, I failed to reach any number of snicks that I like to think I would have pocketed two or three years later. So much for confidence and experience, or lack of it. In spite of everything, however, I was pleased to read a reasonable report on my performance by Jim Swanton. I have liked him ever since! Neville Cardus wasn't so generous, and rightly so. Disappointingly, however, he wrote his report from Manchester! Another lesson learned!

However, not only did England field badly in the match, but they also batted badly on what was a beautiful batting wicket. Only now, as I look back, do I realise that there were only three scores over 15 from our first five batsmen in the match! It seems even more incredible when those batsmen were Hutton, Simpson, Edrich, May and Cowdrey. The injured Compton contributed only two runs in the match. I must say I do not feel quite so guilty now! At the end of the first day Australia were 208 for two; at the end of the second, 503 for six; and just after lunch on the third day, 601 for eight.

Towards the end of the second day I noticed a sign just over the top of the sightscreen. It simply said 'Atlantic Petrol' in huge red letters. I am ashamed to relate that from then on I could think of nothing else but my favourite Cornish beaches and the beautiful Atlantic breakers. Maybe it was a touch of the sun, but my concentration was in tatters - another lesson learned.

There was nothing much to remember about both England's innings, with the exception of a fighting knock from Bill Edrich - although a £100 prize for the first six of the fourth day was surprisingly won by Trevor Bailey. We had been well and truly walloped by an innings and plenty; but strangely there seemed no sense of great disappointment. In fact, there was a peculiar sense of optimism for the next match, even in our darkest hour. Neither was it misplaced, as we now know. Tyson became the 'Typhoon', May and Cowdrey gave England and cricket great batting again. Godfrey Evans came back at his peak with a series of brilliant exhibitions of wicket-keeping. His catching of Neil Harvey off Tyson in the Melbourne Test will never be forgotten by those who saw it. Tom Graveney charmed lovers of fine art; and, as it always will, guile, in the form of Johnny Wardle and Bob Appleyard, gave the team the balance it lacked in the first Test.

In the years that followed I was lucky. I loved cricket and played with and against the best. But those five days in 1954 will forever be with me. Even now, every November 26th my thoughts return to Woolloongabba. I can still smell the heat and taste the salt in my sweat as it rivered its path from my brow. I can hear again the distinctive sounds of Australian cricket and I can see in my mind's eye 'Typhoon' at full speed as he rocketed the ball towards me. Great days. I wish I could really have appreciated them at the time . . . but I do now!

FINALLY STUMPED
Brian Johnston

I first kept wicket when I was eight, and finally gave it up about fifteen years ago. It happened this way.

On Sundays after the war there was no Sunday League cricket. So Test cricketers, both English and from overseas, were available to play in charity games, and I was lucky enough to play with and keep wicket to many of the great bowlers - Lindwall, Miller, Bedser, Trueman, Laker, etc. Then one Sunday I was keeping wicket to Richie Benaud, the Australian captain and leg-spinner. It was at the Dragon School, Oxford, and Richie was bowling his googly, his flipper, his top-spinner and his leg-breaks. There I was crouching behind the timbers, with my nose nearly resting on the bails. I 'read' all his balls perfectly, but most of them went for four byes.

When the last man came in, Richie bowled him a huge leg-break. He rushed down the pitch and missed the ball by miles. It came nicely into my waiting gloves, and with all my old speed - or so I thought - I whipped off the bails and appealed for a stumping. To my delight, the umpire raised his finger. Just think of it. I, an ordinary club cricketer, had stumped someone off the Australian captain.

I felt even more pleased when the bursar at the school came up and said, 'Jolly well stumped.' I blushed modestly. But I froze as he went on: 'And I'd also like to congratulate you on the sporting way you tried to give him time to get back!'

I can take a hint. I never kept wicket again.

UNDER ORDERS
Reg Simpson

Most of the humorous incidents I can recall take very little time to narrate, such as one, with Charlie Harris, the indomitable Notts opening batsman and occasional bowler. During a match against Surrey at The Oval, in a desperate attempt to stop the flood of runs, he loudly proclaimed to the umpire, before the start of one of his overs, that he would try an over without his teeth, which he promptly removed and handed to the astonished official. Unfortunately, the ploy failed to have any effect on the batsmen.

However, I did experience a rather amusing situation which takes a little more space to recount (this has never been told before, I might add). In the late fifties, after the retirement of Bruce Dooland, Notts C.C.C. suffered from having perhaps the worst bowling side that has ever taken part in the County Championship. On occasions our opening attack depended on two local club cricketers.

It became perfectly obvious to us all (ie the players) that the only possible chance of achieving a victory was for the opposition to bat first and hope for a declaration on the last day, which we did our best to engineer by inserting our opponents whenever we won the toss. Unfortunately, this apparently resulted in complaints from members who wanted to see Notts bat first on Saturdays.

Consequently I was called off the field one Monday at 5.30pm to appear before the full committee and was told that, because of these complaints, with which many of them agreed, henceforth I must bat whenever I won the toss. I should imagine that this is the only time in the history of the game that a committee has had the authority to give a captain such instructions.

Incidentally, the match in which I was summoned from the field was won by us on the last day as a result of a declaration by the opposition, who lost the toss and were asked to bat.

Our next game was against Hampshire, whose captain was that extrovert and great sportsman, Colin Ingleby-Mackenzie. I had no hesitation in explaining the ludicrous instructions I had been given and asked him, should I win the toss, whether he would agree to announcing he had won it, irrespective of my decision. To this he readily agreed. I won the toss, asked Hants to bat and again we won the match.

The joys of captains having to cope with interfering committees!

LOST LUGGAGE
Leslie Ames

England were due to play New Zealand at Old Trafford, and I was making my way to Euston for the train to Manchester that would arrive about midnight. I just had time for a quick snack in the station buffet and handed my cricket bag and suitcase to a porter, saying I would see him on the platform in fifteen minutes. On arrival at the platform, there was no sign of the porter. I searched all the goods vans without success, and so had no option but to let the train go without me. Eventually I tracked down the porter, who informed me that he had put my luggage on the Hollyhead Express (needless to say, he received no tip!). The next train left Euston at midnight, due in Manchester at 5.30am. This I caught, but my tale of woe continued.

I think it was at Crewe I decided to have a wash. I removed my jacket, collar and tie, hanging the latter two items on a lamp bracket which was most inconveniently placed above the lavatory pan. The train gave an involuntary shunt and my tie and collar disappeared down the not too clean lavatory. I duly arrived in Manchester with nothing but what I stood in; if there was anyone in the deserted streets who looked less like a Test cricketer, I didn't see them. No buses were running, no shops were open, and it was lashing down with rain. The latter did not depress me, as I thought maybe there will be no play before lunch, thus giving me more time to trace my lost gear.

At last I got a taxi to Old Trafford and poured out my troubles to the Lancashire Secretary. He could not have been more helpful. My missing gear was discovered at Douglas, Isle of Man, but there was no chance of getting it to Old Trafford in time for the match. The Secretary then telephoned George Duckworth, as Lancashire was not playing, and dear old Duckie (we had always been rivals but great friends) was at the ground in no time. By 10.30 I was fixed up with flannels, shirt, boots and Duckworth's wicket-keeping gloves. In spite of everyone's kindness, I was not exactly happy, as I felt this was hardly the right sort of preparation for a Test match, and I was praying that England would win the toss, so sparing me a whole day in the field.

I need not have worried; the rain continued to fall and there was no play. My equipment turned up at about 5.30, so all was well. When play eventually started on the second day of the match, England won the toss and decided to bat. But rain interfered with the game so much, and there was so little play, I never had to take the field after all.

PICTURES FROM AROUND THE WICKET (1)

Dennis Amiss in full flow during his
marathon innings of 203 for England v
West Indies at The Oval, 1976

Colin Cowdrey fluently executing his
favourite shot – the square cover drive
– in 1975, his last season for Kent

Some famous names from the past in this 1970s Old England XI at The Oval: (*back row*) Godfrey Evans, Len Hutton, Arthur Wellard, Denis Compton, Derek Shackleton (*behind*), Charles Palmer, Jack Martin (*behind*), Tony Pawson, Reg Simpson
(*front row*) Roly Jenkins, Jock Livingston, Harold Gimblett

Gathered together to pick the 1965–66 touring side to Australia: (*l to r*) G. O. B. (Gubby) Allen, Alec Bedser, Mike Smith (Captain), Billy Griffith (Secretary of MCC), Doug Insole (Chairman of Selectors), Peter May – all of them Lord's Taverners

Christopher Martin-Jenkins batting for Marlborough v Rugby at Lord's in 1962. He made 56 and 40 in this match, and a bitter-sweet 99 the following year

Surrey skipper Stuart Surridge introduces HM The Queen to Alec Bedser during the match against the South Africans at The Oval in 1955. Flanking Bedser are Peter May and Arthur McIntyre

The fluctuating fortunes of fast bowlers 50 years apart:
(*above*) John Lever clean bowls Surrey's David Thomas in a 1980s John Player League match
(*below*) The great Bill Ponsford is dropped in the slips by H.M. Garland-Wells off the bowling of Alf Gover in Surrey's game against the 1934 Australians. Other fielders: (*l to r*) Tom Barling, Percy Fender, Errol Holmes and wicket-keeper Ted Brooks

HEAD TO HEAD
Dennis Amiss

After being beaten in India in 1972-73 by that great quartet of spinners, Bedi, Chandrasekhar, Prasanna and Venkataraghavan, we - the MCC team - went to play three Tests in Pakistan. We were looking for some better batting wickets after the turning ones on which we had just played in India against four of the best spinners of all time.

The last Test was played at Karachi, having previously drawn the first two on beautiful batting strips at Lahore and Hyderabad in the Sind Desert. On the first day at Karachi riots took place between students and police; bricks and missiles were thrown at everyone and canopies burnt down. The police replied with baton charges and the occasional tear-gas canister. In order to avoid this happening again, the student leaders requested that they ran the security and organisation of the ground instead of the police, and for this they guaranteed no more riots or violence.

On the second day of the Test we therefore had the students running the matches and to everyone's amazement there were very few disturbances, the few that did occur being quickly squashed with the minimum of fuss. However, on the last day they seemed to lose their enthusiasm for the job; before play started we were trying to practise on the outfield and there were spectators walking and running everywhere, with no control whatsoever from the student leaders.

A group of us was attempting to do some fielding practice, which in these conditions was nearly impossible. We were just about to call it a day with the last catch, a pretty high skier from Alan Knott's bat, coming to me, when one of the spectators, out of my view, decided he would also like to catch the ball. We were running from different directions at a fast pace and both looking up. Predictably there was an almighty collision with us hitting one another's heads very hard. The spectator had been wearing glasses, which cut me on the eyebrow. He cut his eye and there was blood everywhere.

I was taken to the dressing-room to be stiched up by a doctor who, with trembling hands, managed to burst some blood vessels with the needle, so there was even more blood over what had been my whites but were now bright red cricketing clothes. After some time he managed to get five stiches into my eyebrow, but at the end of this exercise he started to perspire and suddenly doubled up in pain. Apparently his hernia occasionally popped out and this had just happened again, only this time he was taken to hospital for an operation. Bernard Thomas, our physiotherapist, met him the following year and it seems the unfortunate doctor had to remain in hospital for several months because of complications after the operation.

I am told that the spectator made a satisfactory recovery. As did the writer, who survives to tell the tale.

THE HAMPSHIRE OF PHILIP MEAD
E.W. Swanton

The first two county teams I ever saw were Hampshire and Surrey - or to be exact, I saw Surrey trooping off the field behind two not out batsmen, by name Philip Mead and George Brown. This was at The Oval in 1919. But were Surrey not desperately hard to beat on 'Bosser' Martin's flawless pitches, and were not championship matches in the first post-war summer confined to two days? The answer was yes on both counts. Yet it happened. From my preparatory school in Dulwich I hastened up to Kennington on the tram on Saturday afternoon, arriving as Hampshire completed their victory. This was Surrey's only home defeat of the summer.

It was rather a disappointing start to my cricket watching - and in that I saw no play, it matched a similar deprivation more than half a century later when I journeyed to Bournemouth to see Hampshire, in their last match of the season and my last in

England before retirement from the *Daily Telegraph*, collect the few points they needed to win the County Championship. That was in September 1974 and I suppose that most of you who read this will need no reminding that Richard Gilliat's side spent three days of frustrated idleness surveying a sodden field, while Worcestershire were able to play sufficient cricket to enable them to snatch the title from under their noses.

In the many peace-time summers since my advent as a cricket writer in 1928 I can never have failed to watch Hampshire at least once and often several times. In the good years and the not so good they were usually a side of personality and attraction above the average, led, in my early days, by the dashing, forceful, devil-may-care Lionel, Lord Tennyson, yet depending greatly for their runs on that heavily built, rather ungainly but hugely effective left-hander who summer after summer came waddling in at No 4, collecting his runs with what must have seemed to the toiling bowlers a disheartening impassivity, apparently equally at home with speed, swerve and spin.

My second memory of Hampshiremen is far more glamorous, and it concerns this very pair, Mead and his captain. In 1921, after losing five Tests in a row in Australia and the first two of the ensuing series back at home, England took the field at Headingley under Tennyson (then the Hon L.H.). The latter could not immediately turn the tide of defeat but in one of the more gallant feats of cricket history he made 63 and 36, batting one-handed, because he had split his left hand so badly when fielding that it needed three stiches. Tennyson's attitude to cricket - and, perhaps, life in general - was well expressed by his subsequent comment: 'Some people afterwards asked me why I did not always bat one-handed, as they thought I played much better.' (Australia won that Third Test despite the captain's effort and the 57 and 46 of that other extraordinary personality, George Brown.) The Old Trafford Test was ruined by rain, and there followed England's last chance of redeeming themselves, at The Oval. By now, aged fourteen, my father had made me a Junior Member of Surrey and so in the school holidays I was able to watch my first-ever Test match from behind the bowler's arm and in the select surroundings of The Oval pavilion - a great thrill.

By now, Mead (who as a young man had played for England in both Australia and South Africa before the Great War) was back in the Test side. He had been stodgy on the first evening, but next day when joined by Tennyson he became a new man. I can see just one scene at the start of their partnership as though it happened yesterday. Warwick Armstrong, the Australian captain, was bowling some rather negative slow stuff on or just outside Mead's legs. He let the first three balls of an over go by, whereat Tennyson walked up the pitch and they had a brief chat. Then Mead proceeded to swing the three remaining balls to leg for four apiece. Armstrong, reaching for his sweater from the umpire, promptly took himself off.

Mead was generally reckoned rather a slow player, and he certainly could not compare in attraction with such masters as Hobbs and Woolley. But when the need was there he could press along as speedily as most. Rain on the first day had put England's innings behind the clock, so the need now was apparent. *Wisden* confirms that Mead and Tennyson made 121 together for the 6th wicket in 100 minutes, the dashing captain making only 51 of them. In the two and a half hours of the morning, against Gregory, McDonald, Mailey and Armstrong, Mead scored 109. When the declaration came in mid-afternoon he took out his bat for 182, then the highest innings ever against Australia in England. For the first time since the war, England had the better of a draw, thanks largely to Hampshire. Apart from Mead at the head of the Test averages, Tennyson came third with 57 and Brown fourth with 50.

When at the age of twenty-one I started my life as a cricket writer, Mead, though forty-one, was as prolific a run-maker as he had ever been. It was a prolific summer with Jardine topping the averages and Hobbs exceeding 80, and Ernest Tyldesley, Sutcliffe, Mead and Hendren all over 70 per innings. My own adored Frank Woolley was a mere twelfth on the list with, however, the highest aggregate, a little matter of 3,352 and an average of 61. In contrast with 1987 there were a few very high-class batsmen about! Mead was but one of a handful of household names. His mannerisms were matters for comment and light-hearted imitation. As described by Ian Peebles in *Barclays World of Cricket*, 'he was a batsman of invariable routine in that between each ball he would glance round the field, pluck his cap as if in salutation and shuffle his feet into a somewhat crouching stance.' He would then move into a wide range of strokes, sound, safe and unspectacular. For all his bulk (by this stage of his career) he was always admirably balanced at the moment of impact. The only time he relapsed from complete imperturbability was, strangely enough, in the 90's. This indeed was fairly often since he made 153 hundreds, a number exceeded only by Hobbs, Hendren and Hammond. And, come to that, only Hobbs, Woolley and Hendren bettered his aggregate of 55,061, made between 1905 and his retirement in 1936 just short of his fiftieth birthday.

I am afraid I wished him no good at the end of the 1928 season since, to the astonishment of all, he was suddenly - after having been passed over for six years - chosen to accompany Percy Chapman's team to Australia in preference to Woolley. Thus was ended Frank's then record of 52 consecutive Test appearances. As it turned out, Mead was only chosen for the first Test down under, at Brisbane, which England won by the unbelievable margin of 675 runs, Mead signing off, as it were, with a fine solid innings of 73.

For Hampshire, Philip soldiered on, in company with some of the finest stalwarts a county ever had in Brown, Kennedy and Newman - who bowled virtually unchanged for years - Livsey, his lordship's wicket-keeper and butler, and latterly the slow left-armer, Stuart Boyes. Tennyson's reign as captain lasted fifteen years.

Charles Philip Mead died in hospital at Bournemouth in March 1958 aged seventy-one. For the last ten years of his life he had been totally blind. Yet he was often to be seen at Hampshire matches surrounded by friends and contemporaries, bearing his affliction as might be expected, stoically, uncomplaining. His professional contemporaries were an admirable generation, 'nature's gentlemen' almost to a man, and in that company the subject of these reflections held an honoured place.

CAUSING A RIOT
David Allen

Saturday, January 30, seemed like any other day in the MCC's tour of the West Indies in 1959-60. We arrived at the Queen's Park Oval in Trinidad on the third morning of the match expecting a long day in the field, as on the previous two days we had scored 382 runs and West Indies had replied with 22 for no wicket in the thirty-five minutes' batting they had had on the second evening.

Taking the field that morning we were supported by sailors from the royal yacht *Britannia*, which had docked only a few days before - their cheers drowned by the 30,000 patriotic Trinidadians crowded into the ground, at the time a record crowd for a sporting event in the Caribbean.

In the period to tea I witnessed some of the best fast bowling I have ever seen. On a pitch where Hall and Watson had resorted to an excess of bouncers when everything else had failed to take wickets, both Trueman and Statham kept the ball up to the batsmen and extracted swing through the air and movement off the pitch to an extent we had not seen previously. Sharing six wickets between them, including the scalps of Hunte, Worrell, Sobers and Kanhai, they were helped by some tight fielding and two run outs.

It was the second of these run outs that dismissed Charan Singh, a local favourite who was playing in his first Test. Ted Dexter's sharp return from cover point and the umpire's finger going up signalled the start of the bottle-throwing - and the ensuing riot that caused play to be abandoned for the day.

Initially a few bottles were thrown from the public side; this brought all the fielders to the middle of the ground. As it got uglier Geoff Pullar approached Statham for his advice and was told to get hold of a stump in case he had to defend himself, only to look round to see six players already 'armed'.

Sonny Ramadhin, a great sportsman, joined England captain Peter May and together they approached the crowd to calm them, but they were swept aside by some angry spectators.

It was this moment that convinced Gerry Alexander, the West Indian skipper, who had joined us in the middle just out of reach of the bottles and cans and any other missiles that could be thrown, that nothing else could be done to save the day's cricket, and he asked us to leave the field.

As we departed we were cordoned off by the white hats of the sailors from the royal yacht, a marvellous gesture which saw us to the safety of the dressing-room.

It was a sad day for West Indian cricket, and while the mob rioting lasted, a frightening one. But it was a day also of great fast bowling, no little humour, and bravery from both sides.

UMPIRING PAKISTANI-STYLE
Don Mosey

For something like forty years, stories of Pakistani umpiring decisions had been one of the black jokes of international cricket . . . yarns to be swapped in dark corners by the grizzled veterans of many a tour, with barely repressed shudders. They were digested, with indulgent smiles, by those who had never savoured the delights of Lahore and Karachi, of Hyderabad and Faisalabad. It made a good tale, but it couldn't possibly be all true.

And then, in November 1987, the realisation finally dawned: it *was* true, in all its stark, incredible horror. Television brought pictures of it into our homes for the first time, so it had to be true! And players experiencing it for the first time regretted the occasions when they had scoffed at the old soldiers. Now *they* knew it was all true. 'Catches' behind the stumps when the ball had missed the bat by at least three inches saw disconsolate batsmen on their way; turning deliveries which struck the pad en route to the area of first slip or backward short leg saw a judicial finger raised aloft

55

with an alacrity which surprised even the appealers. There was nothing new in it at all. The only good thing about it was that at last Peter Richardson could walk into the Cricketers' Club, or his local in Kent, with a triumphant grin and say, '*Now* do you believe me? I've been telling you about this for years.'

Men like Donald Carr, Brian Close, Roy Swetman, Jim Parks and a lot more who toured Pakistan in 1955-56 as MCC 'A', could now justify their ceremonial drenching of an umpire called Idris Beg in a bit of horseplay which was harmless enough in the eyes of the tourists but which became something of an international incident at the time. Idris not only bewildered them with a whole series of incomprehensible lbw decisions, but spent all his off-duty time in the Pakistan team's hotel with such regularity that the England players felt sure he was present at the opposition's team talks!

Umpires on the sub-continent have never quite reached the stage of partisan exultation I once saw in a French Rugby League referee - he leaped into the air, waving both arms triumphantly at a touchdown in Perpignan, then placed the kick at goal fifteen yards further in towards the posts than was geographically called for - but a certain relish for dismissal is not unknown. This is not always, in itself, an example of partisanship. It has been known to work both ways.

In 1977, Geoff Cope, playing in his first Test match in Lahore, took two wickets in two balls, then great was his rejoicing as his appeal for a slip catch from the third was approved by an umpire named Khokar, even though the diving Mike Brearley was still sprawling on the ground and the ball was nowhere to be seen. Cope's dance of delight was cut short by the sight of his captain scrambling to his feet and explaining to the umpire that he had not, in fact, made the catch at all. Notably the batsman - Iqbal Qasim, Pakistan's assistant manager in England in 1987 - was already on his way back to the pavilion without protest.

The parallel in Pakistan more recently was Bruce French's stumping-that-never-was with Abdul Qadir as the victim. Unhappily, *he* protested - in the circumstances a natural reaction but still not a desirable one - so England were not alone in their unwillingness to accept decisions. But at least that sort of incident points to incompetence, rather than patriotism, as an explanation for umpiring shortcomings. So long as that remains so, mistakes are bearable. Once we start believing that dismissals result from any more sinister motivation, it will be time for us all to pack up and end touring.

But - please - let us hope our modern gladiators do not claim to be victims of greater misfortunes than their predecessors. I have seen entire England touring parties on the sub-continent reduced to a state of paranoia by the announcement that a certain umpire (Mohammed Ghose) would 'stand' in their next Test, but my broadcast report of this state of affairs led to letters of protest in *The Guardian*. Shame on me! I now await apologies in those same columns by those who have arrived at new-found enlightenment as a result of television coverage. But those horror stories will never be the same again . . . just old hat.

HONOURABLE DISMISSAL
Tom Graveney

I was taking part in a match for the Playing Fields at Arundel in the mid-sixties: the Duke of Edinburgh's XI v the Duke of Norfolk's XI.

Having got a dozen or so runs, I was suddenly faced with Prince Philip bowling his off-spinners round the wicket; he wasn't a bad bowler, incidentally. He bowled one down the leg side and I swept at it, getting a top edge. The fielder at mid-wicket ran round and caught it. I was out - caught Wing Commander Chinnery, bowled His Royal Highness, the Duke of Edinburgh. You can't get out better than that!

I don't know whether it had any bearing on future events, but I was awarded the OBE in the next Honours List!

THE BLACKEST DAY IN ENGLISH CRICKET
S.C. Griffith

The scene, Trinidad, with England facing the Second Test with only eleven of their fourteen players fit to play. The problem was that we had only one recognised opening batsman, namely Jack Robertson of Middlesex.

Our captain, Gubby - now Sir George - Allen, decided to hold a trial with Jack Ikin, Jim Laker and myself facing a new ball attack with as many fast bowlers as he could find. Even Godfrey Evans volunteered! Jack Ikin - a magnificent left-handed middle-order batsman - was opposed to going in first in what he thought, quite rightly, might prove to be 'a wasted asset'. Jim Laker just did not fancy the prospect. I had never played in a Test match before and was determined not to waste such a golden opportunity. I went last to the net and tried as never before, for fear that Gubby might decide to play one of the English Press-men travelling with the team, rather than risk his second wicket-keeper, who normally batted No 8 or 9 for Sussex. With the other two not really trying, I scraped in and found myself about to open for England in my very first Test.

I shall never forget two things about that splendid visit to Trinidad - Godfrey's bowling, and Gubby, for whom I have a great respect and affection, muttering to nobody in particular as Jack Robertson and I went out to bat: 'This is the blackest day in English cricket!'

[The author omits to mention that *Wisden* records that S. C. Griffith made 140 in this his first innings in Test cricket.]

A TESTING TIME
Hubert Doggart

Once upon a time - no, come off it, it was the 31st of May and an inglorious 1st of June 1950 - a game of cricket took place that was neither what it was cracked up to be, a Test trial that told the selectors very much, nor what I readily conjure up for pleasure in the watches of the night.

The match took place at Park Avenue, Bradford, and did not continue into the second half of the second day, let alone the third day. As I was captain of the losing side, for some time I harboured misgivings about the town's parentage. But time is a great healer, and it heals even wounds inflicted by what *Wisden* called 'the sporting Bradford turf' - it had been exposed to overnight rain - and by the remarkable spin bowling of James Charles Laker.

The Bradford story has never been fully told from the Cambridge viewpoint, as far as I know. It begins with the receipt of a letter from the Chairman of Selectors, R.E.S. Wyatt, by five undergraduates still in residence. Four were at Cambridge - in alphabetical order: John Dewes, Hubert Doggart, Peter May and David Sheppard - and one was at Oxford, Donald Carr, who had played in the Victory Test at Lord's in 1945. The letter was an invitation to play in a Test trial at Bradford, a new experience on which we ventured with all the enthusiasm of young aspirants to fame.

There were two problems to be faced before Jim was to weave his spell and work his magic. The first concerned Peter May - to become, in J.J. Warr's felicitous phrase, 'the supreme professional in the ranks of amateurs, just as Denis Compton was the supreme amateur in the ranks of the professionals.' His first-year examinations clashed with the trial and he thus needed the authorities to show flexibility and an understanding of sport, which alas! is found all too rarely today. These they showed and Peter was allowed to sit the papers early, in the privacy of the house of my tutor at King's, Patrick Wilkinson, and his co-operative wife, Sydney, being let out at night, like some faithful bloodhound on a leash, for fresh air and exercise.

No wonder, in retrospect, that batting proved hard for him, as for the rest of us, on a ground which in the event seemed to us like neither a Park nor an Avenue, but rather a Roman amphitheatre, in which Jim would play the role of the lion. As for Peter, I had to swear, on Scout's honour, as it were, to stay with him on the journey and in the hotel to ensure that no illicit telephone calls were made to friends sitting the same papers as him. I can imagine nobody less likely to cheat the authorities than Peter May!

The second problem concerned the logistics of our journey from Cambridge to Bradford and the authorities' belief that an extra supervisor was needed while Peter was within hailing distance of Cambridge. Thus a retired academic coach was given what he thought was a great thrill in his declining years, that of accompanying four Cambridge cricketers a mere step from Test honours to Peterborough, where we were to catch our fast train to the north.

We arrived at a fairly late hour and I vividly recall meeting at Bradford station Don Kenyon, who may well have had a far less easy journey than we had had and whose expression showed it.

This is not the place to expand on the challenge facing a relatively inexperienced captain at top level as he tries, before critical observers, to oppose the pick of England - both to captain tactically and to give all players in his side a fair chance of impressing the selectors. Suffice to say that Norman Yardley, on winning the toss, put the Rest in to bat, and that the Rest were bowled out for the lowest total in a match of representative class. The 27 surpassed, if that is the right word, the previous record of 30, made twice by South Africa, once at Port Elizabeth in 1896 and the other time at Edgbaston in 1924. 'O my Gilligan and Tate of long ago'.

Jim Laker, of the perfect action and gentle presence, unbelievably took 8 for 2, figures that he would later claim on television (during the interval of a Sunday League match) could so easily have been 8 for 0 . . . since he gave Eric Bedser, his Surrey team-mate, one off the mark, and the second run, scored by Fred Trueman, came from a misfield.

Len Hutton gave what *Wisden* called 'a dazzling display of batsmanship on a difficult pitch' before being bowled by Trueman for 85. With useful support from Bill Edrich, John Dewes and Reg Simpson, Len was the architect of England's 229. In the Rest's second innings, Eric Hollies, who two years earlier had bowled The Don for 0 in his final Test, 'turned the ball sharply and varied flight and pace well', taking 6 for 28. It had been a far cry from the Fenners wicket, so lovingly prepared, in the interests of batsmen and bowlers alike (for they had to perform really well to succeed) by Cyril Coote.

As we sat in our dressing-room at the end of the match - it was 2.30 on the second day! - we began to talk about cricketers born in the Reading area. Tom Dollery, the first professional captain to win the Championship, was one. Peter May was another. Ken Barrington was not mentioned since he did not make his debut till 1951. And then Eric Bedser, who was sitting diagonally across the changing-room from me - Alec, Eric's twin was in the other changing-room - said that he had been born in the Reading area. The Rest's captain, a trifle dispirited after our experience, registered Eric's claim with his addled brain. He looked away from the floor and towards Eric, and with a startling sense of curiosity asked him:

'And where was Alec born?'

These Bedsers, as is well known, have a habit of rising to the occasion. Eric looked over to me with a certain wry amusement and spoke these clinching words: 'Mother didn't have a bicycle, you know.'

Some match! Some memories!

PAINFUL MEMORY
Roy Virgin

Whilst playing for Somerset against the West Indians I was struck on the inner thigh (the ball somehow always manages to miss the thigh pad) by a delivery from Wes Hall, the great fast bowler, and it hurt like hell. However, in keeping with my training and the then current theory that you should never show the bowler he has hurt you as this only encourages him, I tried to look casual and as if it was nothing.

Wes, who always finished about three yards away on the completion of his follow-through, was a quite intimidating sight as he was invariably giving you 'the stare', with his medallion still swinging wildly from side to side as it hung from his neck. On this occasion the stare suddenly changed into a great beaming smile as he told me, 'Rub it, man, I know it hurts!' I was only too happy to oblige and it's a line I shall never forget.

CAPTAIN'S PREDICTIONS
John Barclay

Sussex cricket has for years been noted for its unpredictability and mild eccentricity. In 1980, at the end of a hard season, the Sussex team competed for the Fenner Trophy as part of the traditional Scarborough Festival. Our opponents in the opening 50-overs match of the tournament were Leicestershire, who decided to bat first. Despite the class of Davison, Gower, Clift, Tolchard and others, they made a mess of things and could only scramble their way to the rather feeble score of 173 in the allotted overs.

Sussex, confident as ever, set about this target with the gusto you would expect from openers Wessels and Mendis who rattled up 25 runs off the first two overs. It was at this point that Arnold Long, the Sussex captain, came out with the immortal words, 'If we keep going like this, it'll all be over by tea.' It is sad to relate that the game *was* over by tea, Leicestershire winning by a record margin of 121 runs as Sussex were bowled out for 52.

In cricket, you can never tell what's going to happen next, especially when Sussex is involved.

OVAL FANTASY
David Frith

Test cricket is documented in great detail thanks to newspaper reports, radio tapes, video recordings, and books of players' memoirs. There seems, therefore, little that might be added to this mass of data, especially in the case of the more famous matches.

However, on the extraordinary final day of the England v Australia Test match at The Oval in 1968, although I was there only in the capacity of dogsbody for a news agency, I kept scribbling down notes, just for something to do. Twenty years on, they give an unconventional view of a famous event. Pieces of the raw material assemble to give a picture of a day's cricket still unsurpassed for high drama:

"We ran through all the emotions during that last day. Our sense of justice was badly offended when the torrential downpour at lunchtime seemed to have rescued Australia yet again, giving them a series which England deserved to share and probably to win. I shall never forget the hysterical laughter which issued from the Australian end of the Press-box. It continued loud and long, and did nothing to assuage our disappointment as we watched the fat and furious globules of water crash into the newly-formed puddles and trickle down a wall of the Press-box. The lightning flashed and the thunder rumbled, and it really seemed that the gods were having a go at us. 'Send her down, Huey!' shrieked the Aussies, and one of them led the way by cabling home confidently that the match was washed out, and the series thus went one-nil to the tourists.

The score was 86 for five, Inverarity and Jarman in, and Australia 266 runs away from victory. I went on schedule to the telephone room. Through the rear window I saw a newspaper placard: 'Princess Marina Dead'. The bell rang and the *Birmingham Mail* copy-typist said unemotionally, 'When you're ready, dear.' Bill Wanklyn's lunchtime story concluded with the cruellest irony: 'It only looked like being a light shower.' People were scuttling from awning to awning, newspapers held protectively, many retreating through the Hobbs Gates, hailing cabs, jumping into buses, and diving down into the tube station at the end of the road.

I spent most of this Test match seated beside Jack Fingleton, whose moods varied, but seemed to improve hardly at all. The inane chatter of the GPO telephonists behind us didn't help.

During the match I had phoned through Sir Learie Constantine's story and Brian Scovell's report for the *Daily Sketch*, and dashed into Fleet Street to deliver J.M. Kilburn's handwritten story to the *Yorkshire Post*. Among the writers I had spoken with, Lyn Wellings had been interesting. He said there was precious little money in writing books, considering the time and labour involved. Ian Wooldridge later agreed that it is sometimes an essential enterprise if one is to promote one's capabilities. John Edrich, whose book I was writing, had batted all through the opening day for 130 not out. I would like to think my wife and I played our part by arranging to mind little Cathryn, allowing Judy Edrich to be at The Oval to give a touch of wifely support.

Frank Tyson sat puffing one cigar after another, thinking up his four-syllable words. Bill Bowes, who must have pinged down a fair ball in his day, talked entertainingly. Bobby Simpson, recently retired, sat grim-faced throughout. Denis

Compton was rarely seen, except in the Press refreshment room before play. Richie Benaud was busy, from microphone to typewriter to telephone and back again. The big story on Saturday had been E.W. Swanton's conjecture that Basil D'Oliveira would be chosen for the South African tour, that South Africa would object, and that MCC would cancel the tour.

Several million Englishmen wanted to cheer an England win over Australia. It last happened in London fifteen years ago, and that is a frightfully long time. The skies were fairly innocent on the final morning, with a forecast of showers late in the afternoon. Australia, with Lawry and Redpath out, needed a further 339 for victory.

I parked my car off Fentiman Road, and in response to the raucous overtures of the urchin protection gang I mumbled something that sounded like 'I'm a policeman, and don't need my car minded, thank you.' I prayed the warning would work.

The placards pleaded with us to read Constantine in the *Sketch*, Arlott in the *Guardian*, Peter Wilson in the *Mirror*. Touts asked for spare tickets near the Oval tube entrance and offered them for sale further on. The flags fluttered from the gas-holders and the crowd was building up. By the main gates people stood and gazed at the arriving cars, scrutinising every passenger as they drew up.

During the morning session England secured three more wickets, and things were going quite according to plan. Underwood trapped Ian Chappell and issued a warning to the rest by making one ball kick and another shoot. Walters bowed out of a disappointing series with a single. Darting from place to place, I found myself on the top tier of the pavilion when Sheahan clipped Illingworth to mid-wicket and Snow scooped up the catch. Within minutes the staircase was crowded with mournful members as the rain cascaded down and the radio commentators lamented the passing of the game as the puddles widened.

In the Long Room bar men gloomily drank their beer and munched their veal-and-egg pies. John Edrich seemed resigned to the abandonment. That was it, his shoulder-shrug seemed to say. Now for South Africa.

Bob, an old mate, cried for a while on my shoulder. Young Gordon went home, in company with many others. The bars did huge business. Someone reckoned Bill Lawry had been seen with a sumptuous grin on his aquiline face. John Thicknesse looked startled, as is his custom. Keith Miller looked pensive.

The rain eased, but what a dreadful sight The Oval presented for the faithful who had remained. An official abandonment had still to be announced, but the first faint sign of hope was the appearance of Cowdrey, in England blazer, tiptoeing around the puddles to examine the pitch and surrounds. There was much consultation and stroking of chins, but the groundstaff worked feverishly as the sun broke through. Volunteers gathered quietly in the outfield and began thrusting the spiked poles into the ground to let the water away. Scores of sacks were laid and rolled and squeezed into reservoirs outside the boundary rope, which had been lost from view when the flood was at its highest. People wandered aimlessly and looked at each other bemusedly. It dawned on some that there might after all be more cricket, however restricted. We had to readjust our thinking again.

Times were suggested. Five o'clock, a quarter to, even half-past four. In the Press-box copy had ceased to flow. Most of us wandered and wondered. The turf in front of the pavilion was moist but hard underneath, a hot week having left the undersoil craving water. The heavy accumulation was sinking fast, absorbed by a hungry earth.

As things were quiet - positively desolatory - in the England dressing-room I took my *World of Cricket* in to get some more signatures. Tom Graveney had his dark-brown eyes fixed on the crossword. Ray Illingworth, despite his troubles with Yorkshire, was in pleasant mood. D'Oliveira willingly signed too. Colin Milburn, his left shoulder still hurting from a blow that morning, chuckled his way through a few lines. Colin Cowdrey was as serene as ever. John Snow sat alone, boyish and glum. Another of the younger element, Alan Knott, was

66

stretched out on the seating. He said five wickets were too many to get in so short a time (a 4.45pm resumption had been announced, tea having been taken), and the pitch would be a pudden. Edrich, who knows it better than most, agreed. Derek Underwood wanted to sign the book near the Beckenham CC entry, where apparently he had been given a mention. I steered him to the Kent chapter instead. By the day's end he had earned an entry under Heroes.

The sun was beaming down now, and excitement was building up as the players emerged, an unforeseen miracle. The close fielders crowded in, but the only disturbance to the peaceful scene for some overs was the occasional crow-like call of Inverarity or Jarman as a run was stolen.

Forty of the available 75 minutes had actually passed before England broke through. D'Oliveira got one through Jarman, and there it was: a bail on the ground. He was bowled. When umpire Arthur Fagg stood chatting with the England players as Jarman left the field, Fingo said it was a disgrace. An umpire should remain alone and aloof at all times.

Underwood replaced D'Oliveira at the pavilion end. Mallett, who had batted some time in the first innings, propped the first ball into David Brown's eager hands horribly close at forward short leg. McKenzie survived only to the last ball of the over, when Brown caught him too, off bat and pad. The jubilation in the centre and among the sparse gathering of spectators was special.

Gleeson came in, a comic figure, with about 25 minutes to see out and only Connolly to come after him. There would probably be eight more overs, so quickly did the field change over and so smartly did the bowlers walk back. Illingworth was kept out by Inverarity.

We saw the single-prevention process at the end of the over, but Gleeson, far from being trapped, swept Underwood to the unguarded boundary, and aimed other mighty blows through the infielders, who can only have been drunk with anticipation. There was a very loud appeal last ball of the over, but Charlie Elliott, low over the bails, turned it down.

Gleeson slammed Illingworth straight at Dave Brown, who

was crouching only seven feet from the bat, and he doubled up in pain. Slowly he got to his feet, ready for the next round. The knockout would surely be his if he could stay on his feet. The next ball was edged at catchable height, but Cowdrey was not fine enough at slip: 120 for eight, and the field dispersed for Inverarity. Gleeson at the other end faced Underwood again, hemmed in all round by stooping Englishmen.

Edrich, four feet from the bat, caught a bump-ball. A ball fizzed through. The next was padded away, to a great chorus of shouting. A single off the last ball was strategically refused.

What can happen in 30 balls? Knott ripped off the bails, but an Australian foot remained in its territory. Illingworth bobbed in again, and another ball was safely repelled. There was much patting of the pitch, the wide smears of sawdust a constant reminder of what had happened earlier in the day. A threatening black cloud had now wandered off beyond the gas-holders.

Quarter of an hour left. Underwood to Gleeson, and the second ball really leapt. Underwood changed to around the wicket. Gleeson was not in line to the next one, and over went his off stump, to another outburst of hysteria.

Alan Connolly loped down the steps to the biggest crisis of his life. There were catcalls, but he was wasting no time. It was 5.50pm as he took guard and swept the pitch clear, with sarcastic handclapping echoing round the ground. He played the last ball to leg. Inverarity, close to carrying his bat through the innings, took a single off the fourth ball of the next over, exposing Connolly. The Victorian contrived four leg-byes fine, and kept out the last ball.

Despite later statements that victory came six minutes from the scheduled end of play, my watch, and I'm certain the clock at the Vauxhall end too, showed 5.57pm when Inverarity fell. He played the first ball to Edrich at suicide point; pushed the next off the back foot back to the bowler; and thrust a defensive pad across to the third ball. He was not considered clear of off stump, and the urgent appeal was granted. Inverarity was leg-before for 56, Australia all out 125, England winners by 226 runs almost on the final bell. It was some time later that I caught up with Underwood's figures: 31.3 - 19 - 50 - 7.

Twenty-four hours later England's unlikely victory was submerged by the news of D'Oliveira's omission from the MCC team to South Africa. Quite as sad was the overlooking of jolly 'Ollie' Milburn."

Another age of innocence was about to be shoved to one side.

WORDS OF ADVICE
Philip Sharpe

John Murray was always a good pal of mine and I used to look forward to our annual pilgrimage to London and the pleasure of playing cricket at Lord's.

Anybody who has ever listened to a cricket commentary in this country is certainly familiar with the distinctive tones of John Arlott. Also, if you watched John Murray behind the stumps, even for the shortest period of time, you could not have missed seeing him wander over to first slip in between deliveries and have a little chat to Fred Titmus. Time and again, Arlott would be heard to say in those solemn tones of his (try to imagine the 'voice of cricket'):

'And there is John Murray once again, strolling over to first slip to have a word with Fred Titmus, and one wonders whether with the away-swinger to the left-hander he might dispense with third slip . . .'

I observed this myself from the crease on many occasions and decided to ask John what it was all about. I said: 'What the hell *do* you chat to Fred about between each ball? Do you give him advice?'

John replied adamantly: 'Certainly!'

'Like what?' I asked.

'Well,' he said, 'it's usually something like "Quick, Fred, slow left - girl on boundary edge - red knickers!"'

BILL TALLON
Greg Chappell

Bill Tallon, brother of the famous Australian wicket-keeper Don, played a few games for Queensland as a bowler/batsman. He is supposedly responsible for a number of funny stories which have been around the cricket scene in Australia for some time, so I was pleased to meet him at the 'Gabba whilst playing for South Australia against Queensland in the late sixties.

Bill came into the S.A. dressing-room on the invitation of our captain, Les Favell, after the second day's play. I was in a group having a drink when Bill was introduced to us. As Queensland, who had never won the Shield, and still haven't, had started the season well, someone asked his opinion of their chances that year. Bill, who spoke with a stutter, thought about it for a moment, then said: 'Q-Q-Q-Q-Queensland t-t-t-to w-w-w-win the S-S-S-Shield. T-T-T-The only w-w-w-way t-t-t-they c-c-c-could w-w-w-win it is if t-t-t-they r-r-r-raffled it. T-T-T-Then t-t-t-they w-w-w-would have t-t-t-to b-b-b-buy all t-t-t-the b-b-b-bloody t-t-t-tickets!'

I met Bill again a few seasons later when I moved to Brisbane and joined the South Brisbane District Cricket Club. I was made club captain and was playing in a pre-season game against the President's XI when I bumped into Bill.

Over a few beers Bill happened to say that he had captained South's in the past and that as captain he had never lost the toss when it was his call. Thinking I was about to hear something of great value to any captain, I asked Bill to pass on his secret. 'Easy,' he said. 'When the c-c-c-coin went up I called t-t-t-that's it!'

WINE, WOMEN AND SONG
Colin Ingleby-Mackenzie

The secret of Hampshire's Championship victory in 1961 is soon to be revealed. It all started three years before, in August 1958. I had been lucky enough to succeed Desmond Eagar as captain that year and we should have gone straight into the winner's enclosure. As it was we found the perfect recipe for success, even though it was to be another three years before our champagne celebration.

It was traditional that we played Kent at Canterbury during their Festival Week in August. On the first day of the match, Hampshire batted brightly, making 378 for seven declared.

On the Sunday we drove to Highclere, to play in a charity cricket match for Henry Porchester (now Carnavon). I kept wicket, and we were honoured by the presence of Prince Philip, Patron and Twelfth Man of The Lord's Taverners. He scored a very good 30 runs, luckily escaping being caught first ball by Roy Marshall. His Royal Highness thought he had been dropped on purpose, but knowing Roy as well as I do, he did well to get a hand to it!

It was a great day and after an evening of celebration we returned to do battle against Kent, becoming conscious of the real possibility of winning the Championship for the first time ever.

We played ourselves into a strong position on the Monday by enforcing the follow-on, and by close of play that day felt we were about to win a crucial victory. For the first and last time, ever, we decided it might be a good thing to go to bed early,

71

bearing in mind the importance of the next day's play.

We were finally left the comparatively easy task of scoring 82 in 100 minutes. There was no need for panic measures as there was ample time to get this modest total in sensible style. But for some reason nerves started to twitch, and we all went crazy. I was in no small way to blame, for I put myself in early, which was normally the tactic when quick runs were needed, and was soon out! Leo Harrison's cool head saved us in the end, and we scrambled home.

The closing stages were so exciting that I was forced to take a few cocktails to calm my nerves. I was then quickly ushered on to the pavilion roof and put in front of a television camera.

'What is your formula for success?' the interviewer asked me.

'Wine, women and song,' I answered, tongue in cheek.

'Do you impose any special curfew on your team?'

'Certainly,' I said. 'I insist they are in bed by breakfast.'

The television crew were now in fits of laughter, and we were all overjoyed by the sense of the occasion. I was rather offended when the interview was repeated on *Children's Hour,* but with all the purple patches cut out - how are children ever to learn to play cricket properly if they do not know the formula for success?

That television interview has stood me in good stead. It has guaranteed me many overseas tours and the comments I made have served as my philosophy for enjoying the game. It was considered outrageous by some, but accepted by the majority. And, more to the point, three years later we at last won the Championship.

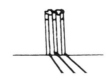

THE TWO SOCIETIES
Peter Loader

There comes a moment in the lives of most of us when we cut the ties with the past. After my thirteen years in first-class cricket and thirteen appearances in Tests for England, after the intensity of international competition and the grind of county play, there had to be some misgivings. What was the real status one country gave me compared with the intimate acceptance I came to know in another? This feeling has no relation to cricket as a game but as a medium of experience. This guided me in judging sectional relationships in one society compared with another society in which relationships were universal. The result had to be the most important decision of my life. In 1963, I became a happy defector from an old society to a new, from England to Australia.

The transition is complete. Not that I am ungrateful for the stimulating opportunities provided me by cricket in England. Nor do I forget the competitive atmosphere in which so many enduring friendships had their origin. Probably I would still be at home - if it was not for my first Test tour of Australia in 1954-55. Here was a vista of first impressions, enough to daze an impressionable new chum, captivated by the warmth of a new and adventurous environment. This was heady stuff, creating a mood that would lead to false judgements about a country and its people. Immediate adjustment is not difficult for one flattered by hospitality, fired by the enthusiasms of a Test tour, and proud in the knowledge that members of an England side are regarded as ambassadors as well as players.

But first impressions became convictions on my second tour of Australia in 1958-59. There was now no doubt about the spontaneity. These were the same robustly uninhibited people I had met four years before. There were no pinpricks of condescension. There was the minor revelation that Australians were interested in me as an individual.

At parties in England I had felt the stilted geniality reserved for professionals, less noticeable when one, as a player, did well. It would be wrong to generalise but there is a stratum of old-world, deep-rooted British snobbery, unshaken by socialism and the Welfare State. As a professional sportsman, one was made aware of the deliberate shallowness of a greeting in the sham handshake, the insincerity of platitudes and the cultivated patronage; a sometimes frosty experience for those who play cricket for a living. But those who maintain this attitude of class-consciousness towards professionals are not always products of an old school tie. There is an inbred British trait that snubs professionalism in sport.

I remember when I left Surrey for Australia in 1963 the team captain, Mickey Stewart, still used the amateurs' dressing-room upstairs, above the professionals' room, a sort of structural symbolism of superiority. And there were other aspects of captaincy in which there was team segregation, not of talent, but of authority. I always felt that if it was possible to choose Australian and English Test teams, on paper, of equal strength, the former usually would win because the side played *with* - not under - a captain.

Richie Benaud, in this regard, was my ideal. He could be informal and articulate. He was tuned in, often sympathetically, to individuals in a team. This gave positive leadership. I remember hearing Benaud, on my second Australian tour, being gently but firmly persuasive with Alan Davidson. The speed demon had been a workhorse that day. He looked wretched with fatigue. But Benaud virtually pulled off his sweater. 'You're the only one who can do it for me, Davo,' was Richie's cajoling rejoinder that overruled Davidson's protest that he had had it. Benaud's outward calm as a captain could have been taken for English-style reserve, but a better word for it would be nonchalance. This vanished only when psychology dictated that he shock a player out of a daydream with a show of refined hostility. The same captain, after an exhausting day in the field, would pour drinks in the dressing-room for teammates. This was an after-the-game tolerance and comradeship in which I believed. Even if it had been bitter all day out in the middle, I had complete release from bitterness after the game.

Fraternisation, for me, included drinks with opponents. Some of these must have been amused when I appeared among them. On the field I could be the notorious hothead, impetuous to the point of explosive temper. Afterwards, I would hate myself. That I should want to share drinks after a game with opponents I had heckled on the field must have proved I was no hypocrite about fraternisation.

Others, of course, on my own side, looked sourly on what seemed like a maudlin cricketing brotherhood. Our skipper, Len Hutton, I was to discover on the 1954-55 tour, did not believe in Benaud's liberalism. Hutton bluntly objected to fraternisation and told me so. The skipper didn't want any good mixers around, playing the role of a *maître d'hôtel*. He summed up his attitude to the enemy with 'You've got to 'ate 'em'. Of course he had good reasons to hate them, having previously taken a battering from the Ray Lindwall-Keith Miller blitz.

Hutton's appointment had been a break with MCC tradition. A professional was captain. But even this famous cricketer, the master (as he was as a batsman), was cautious in the shadow of Lord's and the cricket establishment. Hutton was from Pudsey, typically proud of his Yorkshire accent. But at public functions he would speak with a simulated Oxford accent. As so often happens when one tampers with one's vocal heritage there would be moments of embarrassment when he forgot culture and reverted to more colourful, homespun cricketing usage such as 'ooking and cootin'. He felt the weight of a captain's responsibility and the great national sporting issues at stake. A safety-first attitude to the game became his credo. It could have led to a paralysis of the series but didn't because we were too good for the opposition. Perhaps Hutton was haunted by the possibility of failure of a mission, a lifelong ambition to win the Ashes for England. This insecurity was reflected during the fourth Test in Adelaide in 1955. England was one-up for the rubber and we wanted only 94 on the final day to win the match and clinch the series. Keith Miller took three quick wickets. Hutton was aghast and said to me, 'The boogers have done us.' I was amazed. It was as clear as the Oval's cathedral spire that we would win, which we did.

I always thought, on my second tour of Australia, that our new skipper, the accomplished Peter May, suffered a hangover from Hutton's safety-first doctrine. May played under Hutton on the previous Australian tour. His appointment was a revival of the amateur tradition. He was a product of Charterhouse and Cambridge, conservative to the point of shyness, but a hard competitor. His batsmen could walk if they knew they were out, and often did, but May did not always walk. He awaited the umpire's signal. The tour, unlike the previous series in Australia which England won 3-1, and for which Hutton was rewarded with a knighthood, was to be a bitter reverse for May. Australia won 4-0.

This was a dispiriting rout but, for me, there were compensations. My first impressions of the country had been confirmed, even though I had not seen out the full tour. Neither did Brian Statham. The car in which Brian and I were travelling between Wangaratta and Wagga shot off the road at 80mph at Devil's Corner, where the sign said left curve instead of hairpin bend. We were both in the back seat in that brush with death and hobbled out of the wreck with no bones broken but with torn muscles and bruises.

We were flown home. Arthritis later developed in my left hip. This was probably aggravated by the continual pounding down on the left side which accompanies the motion of the fast right-hand bowler. Five years after the accident, in 1963, English orthopaedic surgeon Bill Tucker told me that if I still had pain after three months I should quit. I was then still with Surrey but later left for Western Australia. I played one game for W.A. against Queensland in the Sheffield Shield competition, and then there was no doubt. The surgeon's advice would have to be accepted.

For a jobless cricketer there was now the challenge of proving to myself whatever I had felt about the promised land.

MAN IN THE MIDDLE
Dickie Bird

Many people forget that I played County cricket for Yorkshire and Leicestershire. They think that I have always been an umpire.

How did I become a County and Test umpire?

When my father died in 1969, I returned to Yorkshire for his funeral. After the funeral I went to watch Yorkshire at Headingley. A few of the Yorkshire cricketers asked me, 'Why don't you go on the First-Class Umpires list?' They also asked me if I missed playing first-class cricket. I said I did. They said that umpiring should be the next best thing to playing the game. Until then I had never given umpiring a thought. I went home and wrote a letter to Lord's, applying to become a first-class umpire. I was accepted in 1969 - that's how it all started.

Umpiring is not easy. It is a job you must try to enjoy. I do think it is the next best thing to playing the game. I always try to enjoy my umpiring because by doing this it helps me to relax.

One or two important things about umpiring: you must have application, dedication, concentration and common sense; you must respect the players and treat them as professional men. If an umpire can gain the respect of the players, that is half the battle. You must also learn to live with your mistakes. If you do make a mistake get it out of your mind quickly, because the most important thing is the next ball being delivered. You are then almost there as an umpire.

When you are out there in the middle so many funny things happen. I remember umpiring in a Test match at Old Trafford when Bob Holland was bowling from my end to Graham Gooch. Graham hit a full toss which came like a bullet straight at me. It hit me right on the ankle and down I went. On to the field came the Australian physio to give me treatment; he came on to a tremendous roar from a full house. After I had received my treatment Bob

Holland thanked me for saving four runs. Graham Gooch, on the other hand, was not very happy because he had lost four runs. It is amazing what can happen in the middle of a Test match.

During another Test - England v West Indies - I urgently wanted to use the toilet, so I stopped the game and said to the players, 'I am very sorry, gentlemen, but nature calls,' and off I ran, to the amusement of the players and a great cheer from the crowd.

I do not think there is anything to compare with Test matches. To me, a Test match is the greatest occasion on the sporting calendar. That being said, one cricket match that will always stand out in my mind was the 1975 World Cup Final between West Indies and Australia at Lord's. West Indies won by 17 runs, but to me it was the greatest game I have ever umpired. Clive Lloyd scored the finest century that I have seen; it had everything - power, grace, and his timing was perfect. I also saw some brilliant fielding from a young lad who had just got into the West Indian team. His name was Viv Richards. He ran out three Australian batsmen with direct hits on the wickets. I have never witnessed a better piece of fielding.

During the 1987 World Cup, which was staged in India and Pakistan, I was ill for three days with a virus. All the England players turned up to see how I was. Allan Lamb, the England batsman, is a practical joker. He visited me in my bedroom eleven times in thirty minutes to see if there was any improvement. When he came a twelfth time, he brought all the guards with him, a small battalion of armed security men rounded up from the hotel corridors. 'Right, men,' barked Lamb, 'let's put this fellow out of his misery. Raise your rifles, take aim, FIRE!' That's Allan Lamb; he's a great character. I think that made me feel better.

SPECIAL ANNOUNCEMENT
Alan Knott

During the 1981 Test match at Old Trafford against Australia, Ian Botham really caught me out with one of his practical jokes. I had just caught Martin Kent, cutting at off-spinner John Emburey. As Dennis Lillee came out to bat, Alan Curtis, who for years has operated the tannoy for Test matches, made an announcement which I didn't hear. I asked Ian about it and when he said that it referred to some record for Dennis Lillee, I started clapping, joining the players and the full house of spectators who were also applauding.

Then Ian revealed: 'You've just obtained the record for wicket-keeping victims against Australia.' A voice from the crowd shouted, 'Stop showing off, Knott!' because I was clapping myself!

FIRST BALL
Mike Gatting

Most people always remember their first ball in Test cricket, whether it is as a batsman or a bowler. I am one of those, although my first ball as a bowler will probably never be forgotten by anyone who saw it.

It happened at Eden Park, Auckland, on the 1977-78 England tour of New Zealand. In those days, I was still classed as an all-rounder, so when the ball was tossed to me to bowl, I was not unduly surprised. Keen to impress, I paced out my run, set a field and moved in to bowl what was intended to be a loosener, to give myself a chance to settle down.

Unfortunately for me the previous bowlers had roughed up the crease to such an extent that when I leapt into my delivery stride, my leading foot failed to get a proper grip on the ground. It slid forward, and instead of transferring my weight to the front, I found myself falling backwards still clutching the ball, before eventually ending up two yards down the wicket towards the batsman, flat on my back and with the team in fits of laughter.

Just to compound my misfortune, Clive Radley's wife, Linda, was there to record the incident for posterity on video, and consequently, I see no chance of my ever being allowed to forget it.

FUN AND FAIRY TALES
Tony Pawson

Once upon a time, top-level cricket abounded with good sportsmanship and humour. In case that seems like a fairy tale after Faisalabad, a few happy memories from the past might be a pleasant change. Umpires then were generally respected because they deserved respect. There was the occasional altercation, of course. In an Oval Test, Keith Miller shook his fist at Frank Lee after his third bellowed appeal was decisively rejected. A word or two passed as well and, with pen poised to write about disgraceful conduct, I enquired later of Frank how the angry comments had been phrased. Frank laughed: 'All Keith said was, "How can you do this to me after I've just given you the winner in the 2.30 race?"' It was a typical bit of Miller fun.

Another unusual altercation occurred at Canterbury when the 1948 Australians played Kent. Our opening bat, Leslie Todd, was close to retirement and, at the end of a long season, in no mood to confront that formidable fast bowler, Ray Lindwall. Ray's opening loosener hit Toddy on the toe with all the Australians from extra cover to long leg joining in

PICTURES FROM AROUND THE WICKET (2)

(All photographs by Roger Kemp)

Sir Donald Bradman in a vintage Rolls-Royce leads the Parade of Veterans at the Bicentenary Test in Sydney, January 1988

A standing ovation for Sunil Gavaskar after his magnificent 188 in the MCC Bicentenary Match at Lord's, August 1987

(*above left*) Two old adversaries, Ted Dexter and Sir Garfield Sobers, putting their fingers up at a Lord's Taverners' match at Oratory School

(*above right*) Bobby Simpson and Colin Milburn make a formidable opening pair for The Lord's Taverners at The Oval

(*below*) Once the scourge of England batsmen, veteran Australian pace bowler Alan Davidson delivers a friendly first ball for Lavinia, Duchess of Norfolk's XI v The Lord's Taverners at Arundel, 1987

One . . . two . . . three for Phillip DeFreitas, playing for Leicestershire v Kent at Canterbury in 1986. His victims (in descending order): Chris Taveré, Derek Underwood, Terry Alderman. In all DeFreitas took 6-21, as well as scoring his maiden first-class century, a performance which clinched his selection for the 1986–87 tour of Australia

(*above left*) Former England fast bowler Fred Rumsey taking a breather at Lord's during a Taverners' match

(*above right*) A familiar face in an unfamiliar position: Godfrey Evans fielding at first slip. Mike Hendrick is the batsman

(*below*) Two great Yorkshiremen, Brian Close and Fred Trueman, for once on opposite sides, in a Lord's Taverners' game at Badminton

the vociferous appeal. When this was instantly rejected, Todd hobbled down the wicket and pleaded that he had in fact been plumb lbw. No matter that his cry for help was ignored. He shouldered arms to the next ball, which sent his middle stump flying, and then declined to take any further part in the match.

There had been some hilarity in our dressing-room before we went in to bat as England had just been all out for 52 at The Oval, and on an easy Canterbury wicket we knew that at least we would do better than England. In the event we were bowled out for 51 . . . that was the only time I have ever been fourth top scorer with one. Never having faced such pace before, I was just thinking to myself that the first ball Lindwall bowled to me looked easy enough, when it was through me with one stump halfway to the wicket-keeper before my bat was down.

Determined not to be caught again by the fast straight yorker with which he greeted new batsmen, in the second innings I curtailed my backlift to three inches and stunned the ball easily enough. Always ready to rub it in, the Aussies near the wicket clapped and called 'Well played, sonny.' Hardly complimentary for a number three batsman to be applauded for surviving one ball! No doubt they were still thinking of an earlier occasion in the season when, as Oxford captain, I strode out to stop the rot at 19 for two. Bill Johnston was the bowler and in his way just as formidable as Lindwall whose tally of Test wickets he matched that year. With his bucking action and whirling arms, Bill's pace varied unnoticed from fast to exceptionally fast and, like many left-arm bowlers, he was capable of prodigious swing while the shine was on the ball. As he didn't know which way it would swing, it was the more unlikely that the batsman would either! My first ball from him started well outside the leg stump and as I tried to turn it to fine leg, it whipped back to remove the off bail. Adding insult to injury, Bill called, 'Sorry about that, skipper. It was meant to be an easy one to get you off the mark.' Heaven knows what his difficult ones were like to play!

On the first day of that match we had removed nine Australians for about half the 721 they had just scored in a

81

day against Essex. Their captain was Lindsay Hassett as the great Don was resting. He was normally a man of great good humour - in a Test match that year he dived into the crowd to borrow a policeman's helmet to put beside him after twice missing skiers at long leg. On this occasion, however, he failed to score and had been sitting mute and glowering at the tea interval. The following morning he looked in an equally bad mood as I consulted him about the roller to be used. 'What have you got?' he demanded. 'The usual light, medium and heavy. What do you want?' 'The spiked roller, of course.' I told him nervously that we didn't possess one. Looking even grimmer, he said, 'Don't tell me you have got us to play at this dump and you don't even have a spiked roller.' As I was in the middle of a profuse apology the smile broke through at last as he put his arm round me and added: 'We only use spiked rollers for breaking up the roads and we ought to be able to dispose of you lot without resort to that!' And so they did.

In that second innings against the Australians at Canterbury, things for a time went rather better. With the ebullient Godfrey Evans making most of them, we put on 71 runs in 32 minutes. Godfrey was then 49 and usually he didn't mind what his score was, so I was not particularly alert for a sharp single, though that year we were probably the fastest pair between the wickets in the country. Godders then pushed Colin McCool straight to the Don at mid-wicket and came charging down the pitch. I sent him back and he was easily run out. 'What were you doing, Tony?' he called as he passed on his disconsolate way to the pavilion. 'Didn't you know that after our first innings a Kent supporter had offered fifty pounds to the first Kent man to make fifty and I wanted to make sure of it.' Next over, Lindwall was recalled and I hooked him straight to Loxton. 'Only did that so you didn't think I was trying to nick your fifty quid,' I told Godfrey. And that remains my story, which may indeed be a fairy tale.

Never a dull moment when Godfrey was playing. On one occasion I was fielding at short leg with Godfrey standing back to the fast bowling of Harding. Cyril Poole of Notts tried to hook and the ball lobbed up off his gloves in a dolly catch to me. Suddenly there was an explosive rush and a gloved hand shot in front of my face as Godfrey snatched the ball one-handed, somersaulting as he fell. 'Why no confidence in me?' I asked in aggrieved tones. 'Nothing to do with that,' said Godders cheerfully. 'This match was getting a bit dull so I had just bet Jack Davies I would be involved in the next wicket. No insult intended, just a fiver won.'

Kent, of course, have a remarkable record of outstanding wicket-keepers and all the wicket-keeping records, good and bad. That includes Frank Woolley's record number of byes in a Test, when he deputised for the injured Ames in the Oval Test of 1934, and Tony Catt's record number of byes in a first-class innings, when Doug Wright on a difficult pitch and incipient illness proved too much for him to take. In 'Hopper' Levett, they also had a near Test-player with a considerable sense of humour. When retired and out of practice he was recalled for a game at the Mote ground in Maidstone. The very quick Norman Harding opened against Somerset's Harold Gimblett, who needed to be removed fast before he scored even faster. In the first over Gimblett touched a ball that carried comfortably to Hopper, standing back. Appeals were strangled as the ball thumped in and out of the gloves. Unabashed, Hopper called cheerfully in a voice which boomed round the ground: 'Sorry about that. In my younger days I could have turned round and caught it in my behind!'

When spinners were as important here as they are in Pakistan or Australia they needed a sense of humour on the bad days. Roly Jenkins had it, even though he was sometimes apt to rail against fate. One story amused us as expressing both sides of his character. It was reported that playing against Scotland, he felt a parson in their team was enjoying more than his share of good fortune. When he escaped again, Roly's language became a little profane. 'Better apologise, Roly,' said his captain. Obediently Roly went down the wicket to say: 'Apologies for the language, Rev, but I'd forgotten you were a parson, because with your flaming luck I would have expected you to be Archbishop of Canterbury.'

Perhaps that was a fairy tale, but I treasure a remark of that delightful man and great spinner of the ball, Jim Sims. I was captaining the East of England against the West. That instantly to be forgotten Festival match at Kingston should, I suppose, have been the highlight of an all too brief playing career, particularly as the 1949 *Wisden* tells me I scored 128 and then 51 in 25 minutes. But the only thing I can recall is Jim's side-of-the-mouth comment after he had taken the first seven wickets in the second innings. I enquired if he had ever taken all ten. 'Never, and it's a main ambition of my life.' When I asked if I could help achieve this, Jim said there was a way I could make sure. 'All it needs is for you to go on to bowl at the other end, skipper.' And so I did, and Jim had his ten wickets for the only time in his career, and we won by 223 runs. That was such a happy ending that perhaps I had better finish there.

WATER SPORTS
John Lever

There are numerous tales to tell about playing in the Essex side of the seventies, with its host of great characters. The problem is finding one that is printable and still humorous when written down!

Ray East is inevitably involved in this story of a trip to Scarborough in late August. The Championship season was behind us and a few beers were being enjoyed each evening with a very sociable Yorkshire side (Boycott wasn't playing!). Ray and I had somewhat overdone the socialising one evening and missed the early morning call for breakfast on the second day. Left at the hotel without a lift to the ground, we decided to walk. The festive mood of the night before lingered on as we entered a shop near to the ground. What was left of our meal allowance was invested in 'Kiss Me Quick' hats, buckets, spades and beach balls, plus a surprise for David Bairstow for spiking our drinks the night before.

The ground was filling up as we wandered in with trousers rolled up and sporting silly hats. The rest of the players were knocking up and looking very professional - until they looked in our direction. Total chaos reigned as the beach balls were introduced on to the field, and the best plan seemed to be to retire for early tea.

Our captain, K.W.R. Fletcher, fully appreciated the reasons for our late arrival - especially when he heard that we had been runners-up in the sandcastle building competition on the beach. The atmosphere was still not quite correct as we started to bat that morning, and not surprisingly I found myself padding up just after lunch. At last my chance had come to get even with Bairstow.

As I walked to the wicket to take guard against Phil Carrick, the comments were flying fast and furiously. Ray East was at the non-striker's end, grinning. Carrick was about to bowl, when I pulled out my recently acquired water pistol and pointed it at him. Behind me he caught sight of the wicket-keeper and first slip rolling around on the ground, soaking wet and laughing. The umpire called 'Dead Ball' and the crowd were left wondering what was going on!

Needless to say, it didn't save me. I was out in the same over!

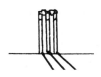

GET ME TO THE CREASE ON TIME
Trevor Bailey

The three Cs provide the best start to an innings. I always tried to arrive at the crease cool, calm and collected and to avoid that unsettling, frantic last-minute dash. Sir Donald Bradman advocated a leisurely stroll to the wicket in order to become accustomed to the light, and this approach certainly paid off handsomely for him.

When Essex were batting, my standard routine was to don an ancient pair of batting trousers at the outset of our innings. If I was number five in the order, I would commence padding up at the fall of the first wicket; not by any means an unusual happening. When the next one went down, I began watching in earnest and my bat, gloves, a roll of chewing gum, and a piece of chiropody felt with a hole cut in the middle to protect the knuckle on the first finger of my right hand, were within easy reach. I wanted to see exactly what was happening out in the middle, hopefully work out where I was most likely to open my account, and to prepare myself for what lay ahead. Apart from then, my viewing was spasmodic. I would normally watch the opening overs to see how the pitch was behaving, or when wickets were tumbling or the batting was exceptional or the situation tense, or when I wanted to study a new bowler or batsman. On tour it was a different matter, because I often had not seen the opposing attack; but playing for my county I normally knew what to expect.

There were, however, many occasions when I was unable to make a measured march out to the middle. At Swansea, one had to negotiate a seemingly endless number of steep, stone steps, which seemed even longer if one returned immediately after, without scoring. There could also be problems reaching the middle within two minutes from the balcony at Lord's, especially if the Long Room was crowded and the door shut. On a number of Essex grounds, it was impossible to see the cricket from the dressing-room, but one learned to recognise instinctively the noise which heralded the fall of a wicket.

In run chases, when every second could be vital, it was frequently necessary to gallop out to the wicket and ignore such niceties as taking guard, or perusing the pitch. Conversely, in gathering gloom and with wickets tumbling, I might well lose my way and ask that most lovable of umpires, the late Alec Skelding, where the middle was. He would simply strike a match!

My most dynamic dash to the crease took place in Southchurch Park against Notts in 1957. There had been no play on the first two days because of heavy rain, and what had now become a one innings match began on the third. Essex were invited to bat, not because the pitch was difficult, as it had been fully covered, but because the visitors fancied chasing rather than setting a target, which now have become common limited-overs tactics. In addition, our attack was tighter and our record for making runs against the clock was good. I then completely misread the situation, not bothering to put on my batting trousers, nor to watch the opening overs. This was understandable as their new-ball pair were not famous for their pace and venom.

It appeared to be the ideal time for our physiotherapist, Harold Dalton, to give me a leisurely massage. As Dickie Dodds and Gordon Barker, our two openers, made their way to the middle I was stretched out on the table in my 'all together', covered in massage cream, completely relaxed and without a care in the world. When Dickie departed for nought in the first over, I was not especially surprised, or worried, but I hurriedly began to put some clothes on when Arthur Jepson claimed his second victim in the same over - Brian Taylor lbw without scoring.

The real dressing-room panic occurred two minutes later, with Doug Insole clean bowled for a duck by Arthur. That I reached the crease during that opening over with the scoreboard reading 0 for 3, and more or less within the permitted two minutes, was entirely due to teamwork. My colleagues strapped on my pads and even laced up my boots in time for me to join a somewhat perplexed Gordon Barker, who, though he had experienced his share of odd happenings with

Essex, had never before seen three wickets tumble in the first over of a match.

Fortunately, normality returned and together we put on 174 to show there was nothing wrong with the pitch, though we were helped by the departure of Arthur with a torn muscle. It also made me wonder whether it might have been better for me if I had always gone out to bat in that fashion, rather than aiming to arrive at the crease, cool, calm and collected. There was no time for nerves or to think about anything except beating that two-minute limit. I simply took guard, discovering that the adrenalin was flowing and began to bat, singing quietly to myself, 'For God's sake, get me to the crease on time.'

ROSES MATCHES
David Lloyd

These affairs are always a little different from the run of the mill county game. When Lancashire played at Headingley, tradition meant that we would always get a lot of stick from the crowd. There were, of course, tell-tale signs of where the banter would start - just little things like people squeezing seven onto a six-seater bench when there was plenty of room in the stand. And at the front a man with a bib-and-braces boiler suit, flat cap and lunch-box on his knee. Nobody would sit within thirty yards of the chap. Intuition said, 'This is where the flak will come from'.

The particular match I recall was not, however, a 'normal' Roses match. It was the first time for quite a while that Lancashire had two overseas players in the team, Farokh Engineer and Clive Lloyd. When Lancs took the field, our friend at the front immediately stood on his seat and shouted, 'Aye, aye, what've we got 'ere? League o' Nations - they're all shapes, colours an' sizes, this lot - an' wot about them two at t'back? Thems not Wigan lads, I can tell thee.'

We were just about to start the day's proceedings when he continued, 'An' where's that from at back o' t'stumps - Turkey?'

As you know, Farokh Engineer could have signed for a host of county clubs before he chose Lancashire, but it was obvious that he knew nothing of the ins and outs of Yorkshire cricket or its policy regarding qualification, as he turned to first slip and said, 'I'll tell you something, I'm glad I didn't sign for this lot!'

HAIR RESTORER
Alec Bedser

I made my first trip to Australia with the MCC in 1946-47, travelling by sea in the *Stirling Castle*, the trip taking three weeks. We journeyed around Australia by train, a really wonderful experience. My twin brother, Eric, was able to make the trip. We had served throughout the war together, so it was great that he too could enjoy Australia. He travelled by sea on a semi-cargo ship called the *Port Hobart*, his journey taking some two weeks longer than mine. We joined up again in Sydney in November 1946.

Being so alike, we had many cases of mistaken identity and this caused a lot of fun. While in Sydney, we decided we needed a haircut. Not being too sure of the standard of hairdressing, I said I would find a barber. This I did, and he proved satisfactory, so Eric went along a few minutes later for his haircut. The barber, on seeing him, said, 'Strike me, mate, I've just cut your bloody hair.' Eric said, 'Yes, I know - it's the stuff you put on it made it grow!'

CHANGE OF PACE
Eric Bedser

In 1946 Surrey played a game against an Old England XI, in aid of the Surrey County Cricket Appeal Fund. The Old England XI was full of great names, including Herbert Sutcliffe, Andy Sandham, Patsy Hendren, Frank Woolley and Maurice Tate. There were some 15,000 spectators and the game was played in a friendly manner. The object being, of course, to let the public see these great players in action.

Frank Woolley made some runs and during his innings Alec and I decided to play a prank on him and on Bert Strudwick, who was the umpire. Alec bowled at fast-medium pace and I bowled off-spinners.

Alec started an over, with me fielding nearby at mid-off. After he had bowled three balls at fast-medium, we switched over without the batsman or umpire noticing and I bowled the next three balls as slow off-breaks. This surprised Frank Woolley, who turned to our wicket-keeper and said, 'This young fellow has a remarkable change of pace.'

THE GREAT MELBOURNE CRICKET GROUND MIRAGE
Keith Miller

I've come across some extraordinary happenings in my cricketing lifetime, but none to equal the third Test match between Australia and England in the 1954-55 season at Melbourne Cricket Ground. This Test I labelled 'The Great Melbourne Cricket Ground Mirage'!

This was a most vital match. Australia had won the first Test at Brisbane by an innings and 154 runs, England the second at Sydney by 38 runs. At Brisbane the English bowlers came in for an unmerciful battering. Bedser 1-131, Statham 2-123, Bailey 3-140, Tyson 1-160, as Australia clocked up a mammoth 601. England crumbled with 190 and 257.

It was in this Test that all eyes centred on England's new speedster, Frank Tyson. The Aussies had had a taste of his searing pace the previous year when they faced him in a county match at Northampton. 'Typhoon Tyson' they nicknamed him. After the hammering handed out to Tyson by the Australians on the placid Brisbane pitch, it didn't take long for the Press to ask: 'Where does a typhoon become a gentle zephyr?' The answer: 'Bowl Tyson on Brisbane's Gabba pitch'.

Now came the Sydney Test! Injury kept me out of this match, but as captain of New South Wales, I knew Tyson would have a pitch that would make things rather torrid for our batsmen. The Sydney pitch was green and grassy, tailor-made for the pacemen. For England, Peter May made 104, while Australia's only sizeable run-getter was Neil Harvey, 92 not out; both batsmen scoring their runs in the second innings. This was Tyson's Test. He finished the match with 10 for 130 - the Typhoon had returned!

Now the series stood one-all with the vital third Test in Melbourne to come. The MCG over the past couple of seasons had become a batsman's nightmare. After only two days' play cracks half an inch wide would suddenly appear. Since the Melbourne Test always started on Boxing Day, it drew enormous crowds and helped fill the coffers of the Australian Cricket Board. From that viewpoint it was essential that this Test should last the five days.

It was these yawning cracks in previous matches that worried officials. In an attempt to combat them the MCG regular groundsman, Bill Vanthoff, was replaced by Jack House. House had built up a high reputation for producing top pitches at a nearby oval. What's more, he put forward a theory to the Melbourne Committee that he could prevent the cracks by using a new rolling and watering technique. Now he had put his reputation well and truly on the line!

Boxing Day dawned, sunny and with high temperatures forecast. A crowd of 64,000 rolled into the Wembley-sized concrete arena.

At the end of the first day, England were all out for 191, with a youngster named Colin Cowdrey making a fine 102. By the end of day two, the match was set dead level: Australia 188 for eight. Midway through the second day, I was out for 7, caught Evans, bowled Statham. I had noticed at this early stage of the match that cracks were already appearing. At stumps, I asked the not out batsman, Ian Johnson, about the state of the pitch. He said, 'The cracks are there all right and some of the deliveries are already keeping a bit on the low side'.

The next day, Sunday, was a rest day. Ray Lindwall and I teamed up and played golf with the then Australian champion, Ossie Pickworth, at the delightful Royal Melbourne course. After playing only nine holes, we called it a day. The official temperature at midday was 105 degrees. Over a beer, I remarked to Lindwall that the cracks in the Test pitch would be widening, to which he replied: 'Just as well Lindsay Hassett isn't playing in this match as he surely would be in danger of disappearing down between the cracks'.

Next day all eyes centred on just how the pitch would play. The not out batsmen, Ian Johnson and Len Maddocks, were clearly untroubled and played with the utmost confidence. The ball came through at normal height and that alone started our tongues wagging as we watched from the dressing-room. After yesterday's heat wave, the ball should have been flying in all directions off the cracks!

Just before lunch, Australia were all out for 231. Unbuckling his pads, Johnson whispered, 'The pitch has been watered'. 'What? Can't be,' I said. 'Sure has,' replied Johnson. All eyes focused on the pitch as we waited for the arrival of the England openers, Hutton and Edrich. There were no cracks! I then scratched the surface of the pitch with my sprigs. Two days earlier the pitch was flint hard. I couldn't believe how easily my sprigs now cut through the moist turf. The pitch *had* been watered!

As I walked off at the lunch break, Percy Beames, one

of Australia's most reputable cricket writers, stopped me and asked the width of the cracks. I put my thumb and forefinger so close together they were almost touching. 'Thanks, that's all I want to know,' said Beames. He then exploded the story of the watering of the pitch.

Beames and I had been old workmates with an oil company before the Second World War. A top all-round sportsman, he was captain of the Melbourne club which uses the MCG as its home ground. Many Melbourne sportsmen who had played under Beames were in those days employed at the Melbourne Cricket Ground and had told Beames of the watering.

All hell then broke loose! Groundsman Jack House denied the pitch had been watered and threatened legal action against the *Melbourne Age* which had printed Beames' story. Members of the Victorian Cricket Association and the Melbourne Cricket Club even tried to get ground staff to swear on affidavit to the effect that no watering had taken place. That was soon dismissed! Later an official denial of the watering was made after a joint meeting and enquiry of the MCG and Victorian Cricket Association. Privately, some officials told close friends (off the record) that watering had taken place. England, batting a second time, found the pitch slow and easy and ran up 279, with Peter May hitting 91.

The heat wave continued, and with the match now a cliff-hanger, a big crowd rolled up to see the final day's play.

The cracks in the pitch had now opened wider and in greater numbers than before the illegal watering. Frank Tyson, bowling at great speed, proved almost unplayable. I had made 6 when Tyson hurled down a real 'fair dinkum' shooter, the ball never leaving the pitch. The following delivery landed in almost the identical spot, reared head high and, more in self-preservation than anything else, I somehow got the bat to the ball, only to snick a slip catch to Bill Edrich.

The big crowd on this final day rocketed the spectator aggregate to 300,270 - a Test match record in Australia. Before lunch the game was over, the ground empty! Tyson had bulldozed Australia out for 111 runs, taking an amazing 7 for 27 off 12.3 overs.

93

The pitch that Jack House built jetted Typhoon Tyson into cricket history!

THE JOYS OF TOURING
Bob Willis

It is almost twenty years since I went abroad on my first cricket tour and I have to say that each one had its fascinations as well as its frustrations. I was a gawky nineteen-year-old when I went to Pakistan with Surrey schoolboys and had my first encounter with flat wickets and overseas umpires who did not share my views on the lbw law. I also picked up a liver complaint that unfortunately flared up whenever I visited the Asian sub-continent (must be my fondness for curries!) and which necessitated my sad, early departure from Pakistan on my last tour as England captain in 1984. No offence, though: the hotels in Pakistan and India are among the best in the world, and the fanaticism for cricket out there cannot fail to warm the heart of the most dedicated Anglophile.

Each of the Test-playing countries has its different characteristics. Sri Lanka is terribly humid - it was very hard work bowling in their inaugural Test against us in 1982 - but astonishingly beautiful. New Zealand is green, verdant and peaceful, the nearest to Britain among the other Test countries. Their players also approach the game in the same way as ourselves, with little of the hyped aggression you encounter across the Tasman Sea. Australia is, I suppose, my favourite of all because there is so much to do - vital for someone like me who does not like sitting around in overpowering heat. Once you get used to the Aussies it is a marvellous place! Their humour is brash, fairly earthy and unsubtle, but they genuinely like the Pommies. Indeed, they pay us a compliment when they slag us off; that means we are honorary Aussies! The scenery in certain

94

areas is breathtaking, the wines very underrated and the meat and fish varied, plentiful and cheap. Definitely the favourite tour for English cricketers: a common language, a shared love of all sports, good hotels, and an excellent transport system that reduces the hanging around for various connections to the bare minimum.

South Africa impressed me when I went there in the early seventies. The discipline among schoolchildren I coached was admirable, the hospitality overwhelming and the sports facilities out of this world. Yet I found there was little to do after dark, presumably for the obvious complications that dog this beautiful country. In contrast, the West Indies is a social animal's delight, especially Barbados, Jamaica and Antigua. It also helps if you have plenty of spare cash, because the Caribbean is now a very expensive place to visit.

In all, I have been to Australia seven times, India three times, Pakistan three times, South Africa twice, Sri Lanka twice, New Zealand three times and the Caribbean five times in my various capacities as player, assistant manager and television commentator. I count myself privileged to have qualified for these trips for the simple reason that I could play cricket. Throughout, I have been aware that English cricket remains highly respected for its tradition, its principles of good sportsmanship and its gallery of great players. I have been proud to wave the flag in some very remote places and, despite the occasional bout of homesickness and moan about the wickets, I trust I have made many friends on these sojourns. Certainly my address book suggests this is so. A cricket tour remains one of the most civilised ways to see the world.

CALLING BOMBAY
Peter Baxter

It seems that I am acquiring a reputation in BBC Radio of being what they used to call an 'old India hand'. Anyway, they keep sending me back there. For a broadcaster, as for a cricketer - and probably for many others - it is a perfect blend of charm and frustration.

My first experience of producing radio commentary from India was in the Gujarati city of Ahmedabad, where Keith Fletcher's team played the first one-day international in 1981. Our broadcasting point was a concrete cave at the back of a stand which was hung with heavy drapes to deaden the echo within and extraneous sound from without and furnished with a temporary window of scratched perspex. The effect was to make the box a suffocating hell.

On the commentary desk we found two or three small and apparently rather ancient microphones attended by three or four engineers from All India Radio, eager to help, but evidently sceptical of our chances of getting through to London for our commentary. Such an ambitious project had apparently never successfully been attempted from Ahmedabad - something of a communications black spot within India, let alone the rest of the world. (My subsequent visit there three years later revealed that this is a reputation they are extremely reluctant to lose.)

As I struggled to make contact with the BBC, or at least with the communications centre in Bombay - the first link in the chain - I realised that our scheduled transmission time had come and by now Christopher Martin-Jenkins in a Broadcasting House studio in London was having to regale his audience with standby records. It was looking like another field day for the Bratislava Radio Symphony Orchestra on *Test Match Special*.

At last I heard a faint voice in my headphones.

'Hello, hello.'

'Yes!' I shouted, with a mixture of triumph and hysteria, 'this is Ahmedabad! Hello, Bombay!'

'Hello, hello,' persisted the voice, as they tend to on the great sub-continent.

'This is Ahmedabad, Bombay,' I cried. 'Can you please put me through to London.'

'Hello, this is Ahmedabad,' said the voice.

'No, it isn't. I am Ahmedabad. You are Bombay. Now can I please speak to London?'

'This is Ahmedabad,' continued the emotionless voice.

'Get your act together, Bombay,' I shouted at the microphone, rapidly losing my cool.

At this point, Tony Lewis, definitely an 'old India hand', tapped me on the shoulder to indicate the Sikh engineer sitting right behind me, just calling into his microphone, 'Hello, this is Ahmedabad'.

The most surprising part of this story is that, shortly after that exchange, we were in touch with the old country. Don Mosey and Tony Lewis took their seats.

'Is this microphone live?' Tony asked the engineer.

'Oh, microphone more than live, sahib,' he was told and he dropped it like a hot potato. For the record, England won that match at Ahmedabad, though it was the last game they were to win on that ill-fated tour.

Three years later, England were to play at a different stadium in that city, built on a barren river bank which looked like a former rubbish tip and which had the distinction of being the only ground I have seen where vultures pass the Press-box at eye level. Fielding at deep fine leg can be a lonely business when those big birds are eyeing you up.

That 1984-85 tour of India enjoyed its crucial turning point for England with the first one-day international, this time in Poona, where a Mike Gatting century restored the winning habit. Sitting in the pavilion commentary position with Mike Selvey, I was approached by two local worthies.

'Hello,' said the first, 'I am a brain surgeon and this is my friend, chartered accountant.'

Slightly bemused, I said to Mike, 'Did we order a brain surgeon and a chartered accountant?'

The other one-day highlight of that tour was the finish-in-the-dark in Cuttack. England were batting second in the match, two days after Christmas, and facing a substantial Indian total. They were making fair progress, but were actually just behind the required overall run-rate as it started to get dark. The England batsmen, Marks and Downton, were offered the light, when to accept would have cost the match. So they batted on and it got darker. Watching from the commentary-box one had as vague an idea as the fielders where the ball was and greatly enjoyed their antics as they ran in circles trying to find it. Marks was run out but the redoubtable Downton was joined by Ellison and at last they got ahead on run-rate. Cowdrey appeared with fresh batting gloves and a message from the keeper of the calculator. But the other members of the Kent intelligentsia had already pointed out to the umpires that another offer of the light would now be viewed more favourably.

The umpires, however, were sufficiently piqued by the rejection of their first offer to keep them out there for another over before even they decided that they could not see and agreed to come off, giving England the victory on run-rate. In the Press-box the problems were just starting as candles were fixed to the typewriter carriages to allow reports to be written. Life is never dull touring the sub-continent.

THREE DAYS IN THE LIFE
OF A PROFESSIONAL CRICKETER
Mike Brearley

Nineteen seventy-eight was my benefit year. It did not begin auspiciously. On January 15 I broke my arm in Pakistan, badly enough to need to have a four-inch steel plate screwed into the ulna. I started playing again in April, scoring 51 in my first innings, but should, I realised later, have waited longer before coming back. My left arm, which ought to dominate for a right-hand batsman, was still weak. I didn't score another 50 until July 7.

'How long would the selectors keep Brearley as England captain?' became an everyday question. One night, while visiting a pub for a bat raffle, I happened to see the end of the 10 o'clock news; only one cricketing item was included - that I had been bowled out in a county match for yet another low score! *Private Eye* suggested that the tune I usually hummed as the bowler ran in was Haydn's Duck Quartet, as that was what I usually scored. One 'fan' wrote to tell me that I must have a hide like a rhinoceros's. But my skin wore thin; it was a long summer, one way and another.

On Wednesday, August 2, Middlesex played at Old Trafford in the Gillette Cup Quarter Final. Lancashire, put in by me, scored 279 for six, Andrew Kennedy making 131. I dropped him when he'd scored about 35. The crowd enjoyed that, and continued to remind me of it as Andy squirted us through point or pulled through mid-wicket for yet another four. When Mike Smith and I went in to bat, the light was very bad. After one over of Colin Croft we went off. More boos (and booze): as we crossed the boundary rope in front of the pavilion a pint mug crashed down from the balcony right beside Mike and me. It wasn't aimed at him, I think. The crowd didn't appreciate being deprived of the spectacle of their southern Christians being thrown to the northern (and West Indian) lions!

Only half an hour's play was possible on Thursday. On Friday I had a benefit match arranged at Amersham, outside London, starting at 5 o'clock. If there were no further delays, the seven or eight of us could make it from Manchester.

To cut a long story short, we finished the match between showers. I was out for nine, pressing too hard and too anxiously; we lost by 21 runs. I had to cancel the match at Amersham, which was uninsured. I drove over to thank the organisers for their efforts. By about 10 o'clock, I at last climbed back in the car to drive home. What else could go wrong?

Only one thing: I was caught driving at 55mph on an empty dual carriageway for which the limit was 40mph.

It wasn't all that bad!

THE BLOKE WHO SMASHED THE CAMERA

Nigel Popplewell

Now that I have exchanged the law of Bat and Ball for that of Landlord and Tenant, I am grateful to be given this opportunity to record an event which may have passed unnoticed amongst cricketing purists, but which gained me a certain amount of notoriety around the corridors and classrooms of Taunton School, where I once taught for a couple of winters. The event in question was my appearance on *A Question of Sport*, not in person, but as the perpetrator of an act resulting in a clip of film shown in the 'what happens next' section of the programme.

During August 1984 we were scheduled to play Essex at Chelmsford, and it was a weary and somewhat jaded Somerset XI who dragged themselves up the M4 on a Friday evening. We had unsuccessfully enforced the follow-on against Worcestershire and in consequence spent two whole days in the field under a hot and unsympathetic sun.

The bonus that the Western Festival was over for another year was marred by the prospect of playing a strong Essex XI, against whom I had never played in a winning team.

I travelled with Peter Roebuck and Vic Marks in what was dubbed 'the University Car'. Unlike the rest of the team who spent their in-the-car hours listening to a variety of music, our car preferred the intellectual challenge of Radio 4. Not for us the reggae and calypso favoured by Viv and Joel; those Dire Straits tapes played at full volume by Ian Botham, or the rustic tones of the Wurzels, which reminded Gard and Denning of their Somerset roots - no, it was quiz programmes and Robert Robinson which we sought. I say we, it was invariably Peter and Vic who attempted the answers, and although they were usually wrong, their responses were given with such authority that I could not help but be impressed with their erudition.

Arriving at the County Ground, Chelmsford, the following

morning we were dismayed to find a green wicket and even more so, on winning the toss, to discover that our captain had 'stuck them in'.

The prospect of a third day in a row in the field was not one to gladden our hearts, but we were pulled up short by Peter Roebuck who took us to task for this attitude. We were very privileged to be professional cricketers, he informed us irritatingly, 'lots of people would like to be professional cricketers, people like Ian Carmichael, Tom Stoppard, Mick Jagger . . .'

To which Vic retorted with gentle irony, '. . . Nigel Popplewell. . .'

In fact we had quite a good day, managing to bowl Essex out by mid-afternoon. But during that season we were subject to an absurd rule that 100 overs or so had to be completed during a day's play. I don't know how many of you have been hit on the inner thigh by J.K. at 7.50 on an otherwise tranquil August evening, but I can exclusively reveal to any publicans reading this, that it is not an activity which will seduce their customers away from a couple of pints of Bass and a game of pool!

It also became apparent during that Saturday that the following day's John Player League match was to be televised.

That Sunday was a gloriously sunny day, and although we kept Essex down to a gettable total, we were not optimistic as we returned to the pavilion for tea. The author was chosen to open the innings, for reasons which to this day are not especially clear. However, it was one of those exceedingly rare days when if the ball didn't hit the edge and fly for four, it hit the middle of the bat and went for six. I must confess that I had some luck; as one frustrated Essex seamer declared, 'I had more arse than his missus'. However, since things seemed to be running my way, I decided to press my luck and to have a go at the Essex off-spinner, David Acfield.

The shot itself can only really be satisfactorily described as a swipe (although my father is still under the impression that it was a gloriously cultured off-drive - he hasn't seen the replay either!). On balance I don't think I was taught it either by him, or at that expensive institution in Oxfordshire where I spent my formative cricketing years. It was a shot born of many similar Sunday afternoons where the old adage of the end justifying the means was extremely apt.

However, the result of the shot was that the ball flew with considerable and satisfying velocity just wide of mid-off for a 'one bounce' four. As the ball came back the Essex captained examined it and muttered something, the gist of which was that there was glass in the ball and that play should not continue until it was removed. I thought it a ploy to upset my concentration, and if it was, it achieved its objective, since I was subsequently dismissed a couple of overs later.

It was not, therefore, until I reached the dressing-room that I realised that the ball had hit a BBC Outside Broadcast Unit camera and shattered a lens worth several thousand pounds.

I am not saying that I gleaned any satisfaction from doing it, but when I have subsequently been introduced at dinners as 'that bloke who smashed the camera', I have to admit to a small thrill of achievement. Rather than being hailed by posterity as an adequate county professional who slogged usefully on occasion on the off-side, I shall perhaps be remembered for an act of criminal damage which, had it been committed by one of my pupils, would have been rewarded with lines or possibly detention.

The frustrating thing is that I have never seen it, and while I suppose I should really give the BBC a ring to ask for a copy, I must confess that I haven't the gall.

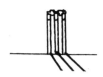

HARD OF HEARING?
Clive Radley

There was always a great deal of good-natured banter in our local Derby with Surrey. Titmus would be chatting to Edrich at the non-striker's end almost until he bowled the ball and, down at the other end, Barrington and Murray would be carrying on a conversation as the ball was on its way!

Middlesex were playing Surrey at Lord's on one particular occasion. The game was fizzling out into a dull old draw when Titmus got a wicket. The next batsman to arrive was Pat Pocock, commonly known as Percy or Perce. Now Perce was by no stretch of the imagination a great batsman, but he always looked the part (nice new bat, clean pads, gloves, cap etc). This time he came out with a brand new pair of spectacles; nobody had seen him with them before, so he knew he was in for a bit of ribbing.

Inevitably, as soon as he arrived at the crease, John Murray enquired as to why he was wearing them. Perce knew what the question was going to be and had a ready-made answer: 'Cos I'm deaf' was his reply.

Titmus hadn't seen Perce arrive and came up to bowl his first ball, stopped in his delivery stride and, peering down the wicket, said: 'What have you got those things on the end of your nose for, Perce?' Once again Percy retorted: 'Cos I'm bloody well deaf, why do you think?'

Now very few people had the last word with Titmus. He got back to his mark, came in and bowled a quick yorker. The leg stump was uprooted. As Percy trudged back disconsolately to the pavilion, Fred whispered to him out of the corner of his mouth: 'Bad luck, Perce, you didn't hear that one too well, did you?'

PLAYING FOR THE LORD'S TAVERNERS
Alf Gover

In the normal Taverners' Sunday games, if one of the opposition appears to be getting too many runs, there is usually someone on hand who can get him out. But it did not work this way in a game at Windsor when a young opening bat was enjoying himself at our expense and not one of the 'main' attack could dislodge him. So when the ball was thrown to me, I complimented the batsman on his good play but added that he would be even better if he picked his bat up much higher. He heeded the advice and over went his castle when I sent down a yorker. After the game he asked me what he did wrong when he was bowled.

'You picked your bat up much too high,' I replied.

'But,' he protested, 'you told me to do so.'

'You can take that as a compliment, son,' I said. 'At my age, that's the only way I could get you out!'

My last Taverners' game was in my Presidential year, 1974. Having attended the majority of the Sunday games during the summer, and successfully dodged the coins thrown when helping in the blanket collection, I accepted an invitation to play in the final match of the season against the Edrich family at Ingham. Mickey Stewart skippered the side and I opened the bowling to Geoff Edrich. The first two deliveries were pushed back, but when the third pitched well outside the off stump, Geoff took a mighty swing, got an inside edge and dragged it on to his stumps - reminding me as he walked out that the last time we had met was in a Surrey v Lancashire game at Old Trafford when exactly the same thing had happened with the third ball of my first over. At the end of the over I took my sweater, but Mickey told me to carry on.

'No,' I replied, 'I'm pulling rank and taking myself off. I can't finish better than one for none.'

YEARS, ALMOST, WITHOUT CRICKET
Michael Melford

My associations with cricket in wartime are so few that I doubt if they justify a decent title such as 'Batting against the Boche', or 'Hitler, Cricket and Me'. But they are few enough to be clearly remembered.

The first was one evening in June 1940 when I had just been posted to my regiment at Whitehill near Bordon. At a garage there, I bought, for £4, what I think was called a two-stroke motorcycle and, being given a few hours' leave, set off to my parents' cottage on the Surrey-Sussex border.

The machine was never to prove reliable and its rider was a novice. I had already learnt that, once started, it should not be allowed to stop, when I came down a hill on the outskirts of Haslemere and tried to turn right alongside a small cricket ground. Alas, the brakes were not up to such a manoeuvre and, fearful of doing anything which might stall the thing, I had to allow it to run its course at its own pace, taking a wide line round the corner and on to the cricket field.

In a wide arc I passed midway between the wickets and I can still remember the look of surprise on the face of one of the batsmen as, having completed one run, he turned for another and found a harassed-looking officer on a motorcycle between him and his partner. Mercifully, before questions could be asked, my course had taken me between slips and wicket-keeper and back on to the road.

The years passed and my next cricket memory is of dining with my colonel one night in another unit's mess somewhere south of Tunis after the campaign there. The conversation touched on cricket, on which the colonel, being a Yorkshireman, was able to speak with confidence. Soon he was wagering £10, no less, that no county since the previous war, or it may have been in the history of cricket, had beaten Yorkshire twice in a season.

He was given a chance to withdraw but he would not budge, whereupon the new APM in the division, whom we were meeting for the first time, said: 'I'm afraid you're going to lose. I happen to know that Gloucestershire did it in 1939 because I was playing.' It was Basil Allen.

I did look forward to seeing cricket at Gezira in 1944 when it was thriving there, but there was no match during my three-day leave in Cairo.

So we come to the immediate aftermath of war and the issue of cricketing equipment, made in India, to units arriving in Austria. A field was found behind the village *Gasthof,* a team was raised from the battery, by this time made up of the original West Riding territorials, strongly reinforced from the Gorbals, and after brief preparations a match was played against Brigade Headquarters.

I remember being rather pleased with the pitch produced by the rolling and mowing detachment supposedly under my command, and it was with a serene mind that I addressed myself to the first ball I had received since 1939.

Here we have to have a flashback to a dark night in Taranto earlier that year, when I fell over a tent peg and put my upper left arm out. I had thought no more about it but when I was offered first ball a half-volley just outside the off-stump, and projected a stroke of rare quality, my left arm went out again and I had to retire hurt.

Demobilised and back on the Surrey-Sussex border in the spring of 1946, I thought it would be nice to offer my services in restoring the village cricket club. I went along to watch a practice match.

Many cricket squares seem to have benefited from having been unused or scarcely used for six summers. Not this one. I watched the first three batsmen being struck on the hands and torso, and when the next was hit on the head by a ball which stood straight up from a length, I decided that there was not much point in negotiating the hazards of 1939 to 1945 if one was going to court even more direct perils in 1946.

On my walk home, I decided to leave my comeback until later in the season. But by then I was no longer free at weekends and the game in that part of Surrey was left to braver men.

JACKERS
Pat Pocock

If anybody could find a way of bottling Robin Jackman's energy, zest and full-hearted commitment, then the future of cricket would be safe for the next century. He believed in the game and he believed in himself. In his early years, he would take a cheap cruise to South Africa each winter and arrive at the dockside with nothing but a couple of cases and a willingness to play cricket with anybody who might be able to improve his game. He loved cricket as he loved life, indeed he rarely drew a distinction. Even the accidents which regularly afflicted him were accepted with the same relish as his triumphs.

Now cricketers are not invariably seen at their best in restaurants, and Robin was no exception. On his first date with Yvonne, the lady he was to marry, he took her to an elegant restaurant and bribed his way to the best table. They were greeted by an unctuous head waiter who made great play of Robin's cricket fame and settled them by the side of the dance floor. Trouble arrived with the soup. As it was set before him, Robin swept open his napkin with a flourish... and discovered, too late, that it was the cloth which contained the croûtons. Small pieces of Robin's toast covered the entire restaurant. They settled on the piano keys, they rattled on the snare drums, they lodged in the singer's hair and they crunched beneath the feet of the shuffling dancers. Even by Jackman's standards it was a spectacular disaster and the tale flew around the county circuit like a newsflash.

It was Robin Jackman who offered me a piece of serious advice when the first thoughts of retirement entered my head. 'Be very certain about it, Perce,' he said. 'You're a long time not playing.'

ABSENTEE AT KENNINGTON
Doug Insole

I was reminiscing with Mickey Stewart recently about 'eccentrics' in the game in our time and, as is not unusual in such conversations, the name of Dickie Dodds was mentioned. Dickie opened the batting for Essex in the 1950s in cavalier fashion, and while hitting the first ball bowled at him for four was almost commonplace for him, he did on certain well-remembered occasions hit very good bowlers for six off the opening delivery of an innings.

He was a bit of a dreamer in the field - a highly intelligent man given to thinking evocative thoughts while whiling away his time in the long grass, so that his captain could seldom be absolutely sure of his whereabouts at any given moment.

The particular recollection of the aforementioned Michael J. Stewart was of a Surrey v Essex match at The Oval, when Geoff Whittaker came in to take strike at the Vauxhall end following the fall of a wicket, to face Ken Preston, who was privileged to have Trevor Bailey and me as his slips - and was entitled to believe that he had Dickie Dodds as his fine leg.

Geoff tickled the first ball he received round the corner, and Bailey and I observed its quite gentle course down towards the Vauxhall stand, expecting our fine-leg fieldsman to be moving in to pounce on it. There was, alas, no sign of Thomas Carter Dodds, and so Trevor and I set off in pursuit of the ball. We were cursing as we ran, but when we got within about thirty yards of the concrete wall that marks the very long boundary at that end of the ground, we were not a little surprised to see Doddsy scrambling over the wall and running full pelt towards us.

The explanation is pretty well as you might have expected. He had popped off for a pee at the fall of the wicket and had taken rather longer than he had envisaged over the whole ghastly operation. He was, as always, full of apologies.

He was not over keen on the expletives that, in the heat

of the moment, were thrown at him, but, tolerant man that he was and is, Dickie put it all down to experience.

BRUISING EXPERIENCE
John Edrich

Having played in over seventy Test matches for England, there are many that stay in my memory - at Leeds in 1965, when I scored 310 not out against New Zealand; my first Test against Australia at Lord's, scoring 120 and being presented to the Queen.

The Test match at Sydney, when we won the Ashes with Ray Illingworth as captain, was without doubt one of the happiest moments of my career. The Test at Sydney when I captained the side, when Mike Denness dropped himself from the team, was not such a happy time for me: we lost the match, Australia regained the Ashes and I collected two broken ribs from Dennis Lillee, the greatest fast bowler I ever played against. Certainly I shall always remember my last Test at Old Trafford in 1977 when Brian Close and I had to fend off the West Indian fast bowlers on the Saturday evening. Having done that successfully, neither of us was ever selected to play for England again. I am sure the selectors thought we were shell-shocked for all time.

Brian was my last opening partner and we were both in our forties at the time. I learned later from Tony Greig, the captain, that we only got the job because, being near the end of our careers, we were both dispensable and, according to Tony, it was in the best interests of English cricket to protect younger players from the likes of Holding, Daniel, Roberts and Croft.

People have often asked me what it was like facing bowlers at over 90mph. My answer has always been the same: one has to make one's mind up quickly whether to duck or hook. I was not interested in hooking very often.

109

When Brian and I walked out to bat on that Saturday evening it was obvious that we were going to be in for a torrid time. I was told afterwards that Bill Alley, one of the umpires and a great Australian wit, said to Lloyd Budd, who was umpiring his first Test, 'Now we shall see the buggers dance about.'

After the first few overs from Roberts and Holding, it was obvious that Bill was right. The wicket was not very good, we had just over an hour to bat and nobody else was interested in coming to the crease. In fact, we were to hear later that after the first few overs were bowled most of the English players left the dressing-room. We never really did discover who was coming in next, though it seems that Alan Knott had drawn the short straw.

Having ducked and dived from short-pitched balls for an over or two, I walked up the pitch to Brian and the conversation went something like this:

EDRICH: What do you think, Brian?
CLOSE: Not much, lad. Good job they're not bowling very fast.
(Nobody bowled fast according to Brian.)
EDRICH: Which end do you prefer, Brian?
CLOSE: It doesn't really matter, lad, there's not a safe end.

A few more overs went by and we were still hanging on:

EDRICH: How is the best way to play this bowling, Brian?
CLOSE: With your chest.

Having played in the 1963 Test against West Indies at Lord's, probably the best team I ever played against, I had watched Brian fend off Wes Hall and Charlie Griffith with his chest and even give them the charge down the wicket. So it came as no surprise to see him once again repeat the performance at Old Trafford. When our ordeal was finally over, we returned to the dressing-room and once again Brian was able to display his bruises, not much different from 1963.

110

Of course the umpires should never have allowed so much concentrated short-pitched bowling, but it gave me the opportunity of being part of an unforgettable piece of cricket and of batting with one of the bravest men ever to have played the game.

BROWT UP REET
Frank Tyson

'Umpire' - now there's a word to conjure with! Author and schoolmaster Harry Altham tells us in his *History of Cricket* that it comes from the French *non pair* meaning 'on neither side'. It was apparently imported into England - together with the concept of an impartial judge of disputed decisions - from across the Channel by Stoneyhurst School after its religious exile in Rouen in the seventeenth century.

In those distant days umpires were, without exception, men of neutral objectivity. Nowadays, however, if we are to believe the Test match tantrums on 'telly', a new generation of 'Ugly Umpires' has been spawned - comparable to anything that Australia produced as players in the seventies. 1987-88 was a bad year for umpires. There was on-the-field Litigation at Lord's between player and arbiter; Conflict at Karachi, Fireworks at Faisalabad, and Larrikinism at Lahore. In the aftermath of these non-couth incidents, umpires have been branded as lacking impartiality and competency. So much so, that cynical francophones firmly believe that *non pair* means that the umpire hasn't got a father!

As a former child of the Central Lancashire League, I deplore the exhibitionist carnival which the modern game has become. When my three stumps were levelled behind my back by some innocuous club bowler, I *always* walked without an argument! There was neither time nor tolerance in northern cricket for actors who wagged fingers at umpires, 'sledged' opponents

111

to rub the afflicted extremity at the risk of being told to 'stop pleasurin' theesen and get on with t'game'. True, we weren't playing amidst the pressures of modern international cricket with its endless farragoes of one-day spectaculars and five-act timeless tragedies; but it was firmly instilled in we youngsters that the game is more important than any individual bravura. We were 'browt up reet'!

The leagues were a searching education, extending from the club kindergarten to the A-levels of a county trial, and it was conducted by stern mentors to whom an excuse was a sign of weakness. Practice was an obligation at Middleton's Towncroft Avenue ground - and there were no exceptions to the rule. In the lower elevens, 'the mosquito brigade's' play and behaviour were monitored by an elder statesman of the game: a gentle martinet whose insistence on protocol was absolute. My own upbringing was entrusted to town alderman Tom Heywood, the skipper of the second eleven. He was aldermanic in rank, stature and demeanour. Avuncular and portly, Tom was almost a supernumerary performer. He never aspired to batting above number ten but would, in rare moments of self-indulgence, permit himself to purvey two or three overs of what E.W. Swanton would describe as 'seemingly guileless round-arm off-spinners'. As a bowler he was in the mould of Sir James Barrie of the Allahakbarries C.C. fame - they were so slow that if he did not like the ball he could go after it and bring it back! Tom's fielding was done mostly with the feet since if he could see the ball he could not reach it - and if he could reach it, he could not see it. Yet for all of his shortcomings Tom was worth more than his considerable weight in gold to the side.

The Heywood authority was benevolent but absolute. His insistence on correct attire was dictatorial and his weekly inspection demanded clean creams, shirt and sweater, and well-sprigged boots. 'If you can't be a cricketer,' he used to say, 'at least look like one!' Today this is a well-worn adage, more honoured in the breach: a situation which would have been unthinkable in Tom's reign. On the field, appeals for lbw or a catch at the wicket from square leg or deep third man invoked an immediate rebuke and a curtain lecture after the game. Such was Alderman Tom Heywood's catechism.

The dressing-room hierarchy was clearly defined. Juniors were the midshipmen of the cricketing wardroom: the lowest of the low. They were the general factotums, one of whose principal duties was to bring foaming jugs of the 'amber fluid' from the nearby pub at the end of a broiling afternoon in the field. Words and tokens of encouragement from team-mates were freely given - when they were earned. On one occasion a Middleton 'pro', the former Yorkshire player Horace Fisher, decided to reward his supporting cast for their help in gaining him an outstanding personal success and a collection from the spectators on the preceding Saturday. He bought a packet of twenty cigarettes to share amongst his colleagues before the beginning of the next game. As they were changing, he solemnly announced the award and doled out a fag per person. When he arrived in front of a young player, newly promoted from the second eleven that week, he paused: 'Nay' exclaimed the cricketing Solomon, 'tha' can't have one. Tha' weren't laikin' last week!'

Such stony-factual assessments were not restricted to the inner sanctum of the dressing-room. League players were confined to the narrow path of reality by the continuous and clearly audible comments of spectators who combined a deep knowledge of the game with a fixed determination to enjoy their afternoon's sport - by airing their views. The headquarters of the critical claque at Towncroft Avenue was 'White Hart Corner': a segment of the ground on the Rochdale Road side, much favoured by those who liked to punctuate their day's spectating with frequent visits to the White Hart pub across the street to oil their vocal cords. The lubricating finished, they returned to their hard benches in a low-roofed whitewashed stand and resumed the role of an unofficial press corps.

I well recall batting in my accustomed position of number eleven - I rarely presumed to any higher status - and being subjected to a rising ball from the opposing Royton fast bowler. The delivery steepled from just short of a length and struck me a crunching blow on the hand, which I had raised to protect my face. The opposing fieldsmen abandoned their

113

claustrophobic cordon around the bat and clustered around me, mistakenly concerned that the ball had struck me on the head. At this injudicious moment I began to shake my injured hand vigorously. Immediately the opposition raised a howl of 'howzat' and since, as I later discovered, the ball had been caught at short leg, I was given my *congé*. As I left the scene of my disaster, a raucous voice from the White Hart corner bellowed, 'That'll larn thee Tyson, next time rub thy 'ead!'

The White Hartites never missed a trick. A late batting partnership between Middleton's fast bowlers Ken Collinge and Cliff Evans - both above 6'4" tall - once produced an umpire's call of 'one short'. 'Wheer?' queried a voice from the white-washed stand, 'I canna' see 'im!'

League cricket is the original school of hard knocks. It is the setting for tough competition, pragmatic appreciation of skill and street-hardened players. When I was 'proing' for Knypersley in the North Staffordshire League in the early fifties, an enemy bowler ran me out whilst I was backing-up too far at the non-striker's end: a stratagem which the Australian Test leg-spinner Bill O'Reilly once confessed that he had never had the opportunity of employing since his adversaries were 'never too keen to get down to the other end.' But I digress; my unconventional downfall incensed my Knypersley team-mates. Fellow opening bowler young Billy Boon approached me on my return to the pavilion. 'Don't worry, Frank,' he stated, 'we'll teach them a thing or two!' He did! When the opposition batted he 'Mankadded' three of the offending bowler's colleagues by hanging on to the ball when they expected him to deliver it!

Character abounded in the northern leagues in my time - and still abounds. Wicket-keepers who stand up to the stumps and take the ball earlier than legally permissible still probably receive a rap over the knuckles from a late cut, together with the batsman's admonition: 'Leave it alone until I've finished with it!' Once a Middleton pro earned a collection by taking his sixth wicket with the last ball of the game. The crowd were streaming out of the gates, but our man was not to be denied his hard-won 'brass'. He dashed to the nearest exit,

114

took off his cap and waved it under the noses of the departing spectators, demanding: 'A collection for me, 6 for 25.' He later explained that it was only 'reet', since it was the lads' beer money!

Our weekend umpires came in all shapes and sizes, were swayed by vacillating tempers and possessed varying and sometimes questionable degrees of cricketing knowledge. But they were worldly-wise and endowed with that greatest of all umpiring attributes: a usually quiet sense of Lancashire humour. On one rare occasion when an umpire was subjected to a player's unsolicited opinion on one of his debatable decisions, he turned calmly towards the agitated one and enquired: 'What's the matter, lad? Has t'wife been givin' you a bad time at 'ome this morning?' The question was redolent with mischievous enjoyment.

Perhaps such a puckish sense of wit is missing from the modern game. It certainly wasn't absent in Len Hutton when Jack Sokell of the Wombwell Cricket Lovers' Society took the England skipper and me to speak to the prisoners of Armley Gaol in Leeds. Before the prison gates clanged shut behind us, Len had drawn me to one side and whispered confidentially: 'At the end of the speeches there is certain to be one question that I want to answer - who is the only first-class cricketer to take a hat-trick of lbws? I've been here a couple of times before!' As predicted, when question-time began, a prisoner at the back of the recreation hall stood up and posed the query. Len rose to his feet immediately and gave the exact answer, chapter and verse. And he added rather unnecessarily before he sat down, 'that bloke was your brother!'

The questioner showed no dissent at Len's uncalled-for footnote to his answer. He did not abuse the prison officers, wag fingers of reproach - he did not even try to break out of gaol! He accepted Len's comment with a wry smile and sat down. Even he had been 'browt up reet'.

IDENTITY PROBLEM
Roy Virgin

Arrangements had been made for the Mayor of Waltham Forest (the local borough) to be introduced to both teams during the Essex v Northants match at Leyton in 1974. Bishan Singh Bedi was a member of the Northants side for this game, having just rejoined us after the completion of the short tour of England by India during the first half of the season.

In that series he had bowled a third of the total overs in the two Test matches and therefore had hardly been off the TV screens, which, in addition to the fact that he always wore a brightly coloured 'patka' on his head when fielding, had made him instantly recognisable to almost everyone. Jim Watts, the Northants captain, came to Bishan in the line-up (on this occasion he was sporting a very distinctive sky blue patka) and calmly introduced him to the Mayor with the words 'and this is Joe Smith'.

As can be imagined, the rest of us could hardly keep a straight face and when the Mayor responded with 'Pleased to meet you, Mr Smith', everyone burst into laughter. To his credit, this eventually included the Mayor as he gradually realised that he had been the victim of a practical joke. Having all enjoyed the moment, the correct introduction was then made.

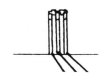

JOKERS DOWN UNDER
Bill Lawry

John Power was a genuine fast bowler for Victoria who unfortunately was never selected for Australia, but in his own right was a great personality.

Power opened the bowling for Victoria one day and at the end of the first over asked John Wildsmith, playing in his first Shield game, to pick up his bowling marker. Young Wildsmith was taken back a step or two when he discoverd that the marker was in fact Power's false teeth!

During the same season Victoria was playing New South Wales, the outstanding team of that decade, in front of a large crowd at the MCG. Power took the wickets of three top-order batsmen in one over, then casually strolled down the wicket to captain Len Maddocks and enquired, 'Were any of them any good?'

My first captain was the great Richie Benaud, a man for whom I have the greatest respect as a captain, player and person. Unfortunately, though, he was always last to be ready for the team bus or reception, and many a time the bus would be held up waiting for him.

The immaculate Benaud was a very slow dresser after the game, and Frank Misson, New South Wales and Australian fast bowler, was always trying to encourage him to hurry up. But to no avail.

In desperation one day we nailed the captain's shoes to the floor of the dressing-room at the Sydney Cricket Ground. All the team watched with hopeful expectation as Benaud slowly got dressed. It was a magic moment when at last he bent down to pick up his shoes. After two unsuccessful attempts, he finally realised what had happened and screamed out, 'Bloody Misson' - which had little effect on Frank or the rest of the team, who were rolling around in tears.

OUT OF PRACTICE
Colin Cowdrey

Denis Compton was a freak. There may have been greater batsmen - not many - but none more innovative and few with such flair for the big occasion.

Happily for me, Denis was still an automatic selection in my early Test matches and was in the side for my first Test in England. This was at Manchester against South Africa in 1955. Ninety thousand people watched over five gloriously sunny days and, in a superb match, South Africa ran out the winners on the fifth evening with just three minutes to spare. There were a number of memorable performances, but Denis Compton's triumphs were quite remarkable.

First, I must give a little background. Denis Compton was never one to spend much time on practice. The England team always met for a light practice at 4pm on the Wednesday, the rest day prior to the Test match. For the stalwarts - Hutton, Compton, Evans, Bedser, Laker, Trueman, Statham - it came as rather a chore. For the youngsters it provided quite a valuable get-together.

This particular season, Compton had appeared very late for practice prior to each of the first two Tests. Gubby Allen, Chairman of Selectors, decided that a little more discipline was required and, with each letter of invitation to play in the Test match, came a pointed command to be at Manchester, changed and ready to practise before 4pm.

At 3.30pm there were ten of us at practice in the nets and much merriment that there be no sign of Compton. Four o'clock came and went - and still no Compton. Gubby Allen and Peter May exchanged glances, disbelieving. When he had not appeared by the time the players left Old Trafford for the hotel, we started to worry that he might have had an accident.

Just before sitting down to the team dinner at eight o'clock, in he walked, a picture of health but hugely embarrassed and muttering apologies. Chairman and captain were relieved to see him in one piece but were conscious of the need to impose some penalty, subject to his explanation.

What an extraordinary story he had to relate.

On the Tuesday, Middlesex had beaten Worcester long before lunch and, with the weather sunny and set fair and his young family ensconced in a sea house at West Wittering, Denis jumped in the car to spend the late afternoon with them. He had calculated that, after an early paddle with the kids in the sea on the Wednesday morning, and a quick breakfast, he could make Manchester well before 4pm.

Alas, the good weather had brought the traffic out and the roads were congested. As he travelled near his home at Gerrards Cross he decided that the solution lay in ditching his car at the house of a good friend with a pilot's licence and hope that he could pop him up into a private aerodrome near Manchester. He was in luck. The pilot was home and was delighted to help, except that he could not take the cricket bag - just space enough for overnight things, and some cricket boots and flannels under his arm. This was a disappointment but at least he could be at Manchester with time to spare.

But the plane ran into turbulence and heavy winds, and they had to come down in Derbyshire for running repairs, which turned out to be something a little more complicated. He summoned a taxi and, although the time for practice had long since gone, he was safely delivered to the hotel in time for dinner. Here he was, profuse with his apologies, and much embarrassed to arrive for a major Test match without his cricket bag.

It was difficult to be angry with Denis, for he never wittingly set out to let anyone down. Gubby Allen read the riot act, instructing him to be on the Old Trafford Ground at 9am, where the secretary, Geoffrey Howard - good friend to us all - would do his best to find some cricket clothing.

I can see him now, unearthing from Fred Titmus's bag a tatty, walnut-coloured antique Gunn & Moore. By the end of the day England had been bowled out for 284, Compton (with the Titmus bat) had scored 158. It was a remarkable batting performance against a hostile attack - Heine and Adcock, with Goddard and Tayfield in support. I felt proud to have been on the same scoreboard; but, in the second innings, he went on to produce the greatest Compton cameo that I ever saw. In an hour and a half he devastated the South African attack with 71 astonishing runs. He hit Tayfield for four consecutive fours, every ball identical and to a good length - the first swept behind square, the second lofted over mid-on, the third charged and driven wide of mid-off, the fourth square-driven past cover point's left hand. Tayfield took off his cap, close to tears.

Denis was given a standing ovation. As he reached the dressing-room Freddie Titmus commandeered his bat. After a few minutes, as the excitement died down, Denis was heard to chuckle, without the slightest malice, 'If only I had turned up in time for practice'!

SLEEP PROBLEM
Clive Lloyd

Whenever I made a big score in Test matches and was still batting at the close of play, I could never sleep that night. It was in 1973 and we were playing against England at The Oval. I had made 132 not out by the end of the day and, realising I wouldn't get a lot of sleep that night, I asked our captain, Rohan Kanhai, if he could recommend something to help. He suggested sleeping tablets and gave me some Mogadons. He, of course, did not realise that if you are not accustomed to these tablets they can have a delayed effect. I arrived at the ground the next morning feeling very drowsy, was out first ball, and promptly fell asleep for the rest of the day.

CRICKET AROUND THE WORLD
Derrick Robins

Derrick Robins' XI played more than 200 matches, starting with the Festivals at The Saffrons, Eastbourne. We toured literally all over the world, to West Indies, Australia, Tasmania, New Zealand, The Far East, Hong Kong, Singapore, Malaysia, Sri Lanka, right across Canada, South America - Colombia, Peru, Chile, Argentina and Brazil; but, of course, the most important were the four tours which went to South Africa.

I was particularly disappointed at the disruption which had occurred between world cricket and South Africa. I had arranged to have the first match of the South African tour at Eastbourne despite the fact that the Chief Constable of Sussex clearly did not welcome it. I was a member of the fighting committee under George Newman VC, but all to no avail.

So it was against this background I proposed taking the first English team to South Africa, something which in those days was applauded and supported by the administration at Lord's and by all the county cricket teams. How times have changed. It was Jack Cheetham who provided the bridge in South Africa and we got on like a house on fire, arranging the first tour. The hospitality was quite fantastic and the people of South Africa so appreciative.

Our team consisted of Bob Willis, Mike Smith (Middlesex), Roger Knight, John Lever, Peter Willey, David Hughes, Robin Hobbs, John Hampshire, Frank Hayes, David Turner, Clive Radley, Arnold Long and Peter Lewington. David Brown was captain, with J.T. Murray vice-captain. Jack Bannister was manager, Brian Johnston the PRO and Jack Jennings physiotherapist.

The greatest moment for me, however, occurred on the second South African tour. Minister Piet Koornhof had asked me to bring a team again the following season. I had replied that there was no point in doing so unless it could be a multi-racial team and, further, if I brought such a team, would South Africa put out a multi-racial side against us? He agreed to arrange it

121

and thus it was that our team included two non-whites: John Shepherd of West Indies and Younis Ahmed of Pakistan. South Africa also included two coloured players in their team.

I shall always remember the 'Test' at Newlands - for the S.A.C.U. called them Test matches. In front of a packed house at Newlands, John Shepherd went out to bat against the second new ball, bowled mighty quickly by Mike Procter. The first ball of the over was a bouncer which aroused and excited the black section of the crowd. The next ball John creamed through the covers. The black section now applauded. The fourth ball of the over was another bouncer. John unfortunately slipped and fell on the ground. The black section were now really agitated, annoyed and running onto the field. The fifth ball, God bless him, John hit for an enormous six. Order had to be restored amid loud applause.

And then came the great moment. John played a single off the last ball of the over and arrived at Mike Procter's end, whereupon Mike put his arm around John's shoulders and they went off having a jolly good laugh. Sixteen thousand people in the stadium were absolutely silent; they had never seen it before, a white man putting his arm around a black man *in public*. It was but a few minutes before close of play and a number of the committee members in the Long Room afterwards were close to tears, saying it was the finest and loveliest moment they had ever seen in South African cricket - and it certainly was for me too. My contribution, in a small way, to start mixing everyone in South African cricket. Multi-racial cricket is now an everyday occurrence almost everywhere in the country.

When one thinks about the other tours it always seems to bring to mind personalities. Our Far East tour finished in Sri Lanka. One day I found the manager of the hotel in Kandi in a very agitated mood, asking if I would go and see one of the bedrooms. I knew exactly which one it would be; and so it proved. The sight was alarming. Thousands of red ball marks on the white walls, ceiling, everywhere. Chris Cowdrey and David Gower, both very young men at the time, had been playing a 'Test match' which apparently had been going on from 11pm until about 4am. I waited in their room for their return and they were, of course, very apologetic and immediately paid for the damage, which the manager had assessed at 100 rupees - approximately £9. It would have cost about £900 in England.

We were entertained on one occasion during the Far East tour in a little village hall. It was an event of no particular official significance, but very pleasantly organised. One of the villagers got up to make an impromptu speech from the stage of the hall, but he just could not stop talking. After what seemed a very long time, when politeness was completely exhausted, the curtains started to close from either side of the stage, enveloping the little man who promptly disappeared from view. Two of the younger members of the team had saved the day.

On our first tour to South Africa, my dear friend Brian Johnston acted as our PRO and what a terrific job he made of it. The tour song was the old music-hall number 'On Mother Kelly's Doorstep'. One day at the Tollman Towers Hotel in Johannesburg, I was sitting in the lounge with Brian and the actor David Tomlinson. A pianist was performing and he looked pretty old fashioned in morning coat and wing collar. He was quietly strumming through Noel Coward and Ivor Novello, with a bit of Chopin thrown in. Brian announced he felt certain the pianist would know 'On Mother Kelly's Doorstep'. A more unlikely thought could not be imagined and Tomlinson and I immediately disagreed with Johnston, whereupon bets were laid: five to one that the pianist would not know the song. We went across to the pianist and made our request. He played the tune without hesitation. Many drinks later, and after much persuading, Johnners confessed. The tune was also the theme song of M.J.K. Smith's 1964 tour, when the pianist was at the Edward Hotel in Durban, and the tourists had taught it to him. Just typical of the lovely nonsense Johnners seems to manufacture wherever he goes.

One of our most interesting tours was to the West Indies, where we played in some fourteen different islands. We went on the basis that we all paid all our own expenses but any money taken from a gate of over 5,000 would be divided 50-50. It was astonishing how many gates there were of 4,900 to 4,999. We finally played a match at Antigua against the Combined Islands with something like 15,000 people in the ground, but we still made no profit. 'There have been some extraneous and expensive expenses' our manager, Les Ames, was told. Les, by this time, was getting cheesed off and asked to see the accounts. He queried one large figure and was told it was the cost of 'painting the pavilion'. When you got to that stage, you just had no chance.

Gate money aside, it was not a very happy tour. Placards and headlines such as 'Robins take your South Africans back to South Africa' greeted us in many places, which was rather annoying because every one of our team was an English county player.

In Canada also we had our South African problems. Demonstrations took place at Edmonton, the scene some twelve months later of the Commonwealth Games. On a very sunny day demonstrators took tin foil to the sightscreens and flashed it into the eyes of our opening batsmen, David Gower and Bill Athey, who replied at lunchtime with 204 runs for no wicket!

Canadian cricket is the scene of a great revolution. Apart from Vancouver, Victoria Island and Toronto, all the other fourteen places we played in had a cricket team consisting of never more than two whites, with the rest West Indians or Asians.

It was recommended by Lord's that we should stay in billets rather than hotels, but after a week or so I sensed a little uneasiness among the members of the team. I asked John Barclay how things were going, and for instance, what had he been served for breakfast that day. A plateful of eggs, bacon, sausage, potatoes and waffles, was the reply - 'the whole bloody lot covered in maple syrup.' I asked what his West Indian host had for his breakfast. 'A large glass of rum,' said John. We moved into hotels shortly afterwards.

On this particular tour I had to get permission from the Treasury to take money out of England. It was during the time of exchange control restrictions. The Treasury, in allowing me to take the money out, stated that I had to account for every penny. Peter Parfitt and I played golf at a wonderful new course recently laid out by Jack Nicklaus, having previously been to the bank and drawn out the equivalent of £5,000. At the end of the game and halfway home in a taxi, I suddenly realised I had not got the money. We raced back to the golf club and after much turmoil it was discovered at the bottom of my golf bag. The interesting point which Parf made to me as we desperately searched for the money was, how would I explain the loss to the Treasury? Would they accept '£5,000 presumably lost on a golf course'? Presumably not!

Of our many cricket matches over the years, our greatest win was clearly beating Rohan Kanhai's West Indian touring team of 1973 by ten wickets. It was their only defeat during that tour of England. The strangest result was against the RAF side, captained by Maurice Fenner. I had what might be considered far too strong a team for the RAF - Garry Sobers, Seymour Nurse, Peter Lashley, Bob Gale, J.T. Murray, Jim Laker etc. Maurice's opening comment was, 'Well, we can't possibly make a game of it.' I told him not to worry and said I'd make sure it finished at 6pm on the last day. I was quite wrong. Bob Wilson and I arrived at the wicket in the second innings at 2.30pm with the score at 59 for nine. We were all out an hour later for 96, and were beaten by eight wickets. You never know with cricket.

There was an amusing episode when Rohan Kanhai was playing for my XI against the RAF on another occasion. Rohan was out for a duck in his first innings, dragging a ball from a very ordinary left-arm bowler on to his wicket. At the bar in the evening the bowler was foolish enough to say to Rohan, 'You know, I dreamt I was going to bowl you for nought.' Not the most tactful thing to say, particularly to Rohan, whose face was a picture, but he quietly replied, 'Keep dreaming, boy, keep dreaming.' In the second innings he and Hylton Ackerman were winning the match for us when the skipper of the RAF, Alan Shirreff, who has a good sense of humour, decided to put the left-arm bowler on to bowl the last over to Rohan. His first ball was hit for one of the most enormous sixes I have ever seen - very nearly into the high street of Leamington Spa.

Rohan called up the wicket: 'Dreamer boy, I hope that gives you a bloody nightmare.'

My cricket tours have now finished, and at my age you grow further and further away from the players. But the memories linger on. Sport, especially cricket, has given me so much enjoyment. To use a phrase from that very famous calypso:

> *Cricket, lovely cricket,*
> *At Lord's where I saw it . . .*

And a lot of other places, too.

THE NEW LORD'S TAVERNERS
CRICKET QUIZ BOOK
Compiled by Graham Tarrant
Foreword by Allan Border

Who is the only Australian captain to have twice regained the Ashes?
Which of the three 'Ws' scored the most Test hundreds?
Who holds the record for the most appearances in one-day internationals?
Who was recalled to Pakistan's Test team after an absence of 17 years?
When did two 'GPs' last open the innings for England?

500 or more questions and answers to challenge, inform and entertain cricket fans, young and old. From Abel to Zulfiqar, from Hambledon to Hyderabad – it's all a question of cricket.

SUNSHINE, SIXES AND CIDER
A History of Somerset Cricket Club
David Foot

David Foot, well-known cricket journalist and author, here provides the complete history of Somerset Cricket Club, stretching back well over 100 years. It is a sparkling *human* record, laced with anecdote, humour, social history and pavilion politics, that spans the generations. It also contains invaluable up-to-date statistical appendices.